Lost Sense of Self & the Ethics Crisis

Learn to Live and Work Ethically

By

Paul P. Jesep, JD, MPS, MA

Ethics is nothing else than reverence for life.

Albert Schweitzer

A publication of:

Entrepreneur Spirit

©Paul P. Jesep 2012.
www.EntrepreneurSpirit.biz

Acknowledgements

Friends and colleagues provided important support, feedback, and encouragement. Any errors that may exist are solely mine.

I'm grateful for the time, input, and excellent counsel of: Andrew Bigness, Mary Lou Higgins, David Hochman, Dan Moran, Sue Speir, and Kathy Wise.

The seed for this project was planted many years ago. One of my professional experiences taught me that *if board directors are disengaged or think an executive or senior manager is too valuable to be fired for indiscretions then ethics in the workplace doesn't stand a chance.* It reminds me of an old New England expression: "When a fish rots it rots from the head down."

The book was first suggested by Dan Moran, President of Next-Act. He identified unaddressed areas in the ongoing discussion about personal and professional ethics. Mr. Moran saw the need for broadening the discussion about ethics and probing why personal and professional indiscretions seem epidemic. He played a very important part in this project.

Katy Wise is an editor's editor. Her policy prowess and technical insights were invaluable. During the year long process to craft the manuscript my stomach and mind were also fueled by the wonderful cuisine of Sue Speir. I also had the benefit of long conversations with both drawing on their policy and business acumen.

Mary Lou Higgins, an exceptional editor, had the patience to read several drafts of the manuscript with the same enthusiasm as if doing it for the first time. Her valued and invaluable contributions are evident throughout the book. In addition, I had the benefit of her personal and professional insights over many conversations while enjoying numerous pots of fresh brewed tea.

David Hochman, a gracious, thoughtful, and seasoned business leader in the high tech community, provided both macro and micro observations that we were very important in improving the quality of the manuscript. He was the first person to offer feedback and in hindsight was rather kind in his comments. The quality of his expertise cannot be overstated.

Lastly, Andrew Bigness shared his wit and soft sarcasm that assisted in keeping my sanity during this arduous process.

Dedication

This book is dedicated to board directors who treat senior executives that engage in wrongdoing with the same standards as those who work on the front line.

It is dedicated to men and women of character who don't justify or rationalize the bad, inept behavior of senior staff because of contractual or financial considerations.

This book is for board directors who don't throw up their hands thinking that they were too removed from a situation to press for a fair, transparent investigation no matter where the facts may lead.

It is for men and women who have an interest in the whole organization and take the time to know its ethical culture even when the budget or financial numbers look good on paper. These are dedicated professionals who understand the big picture.

This book is for board directors that use their authority to correct abuse that can and does exist in the workplace. Although there is tragedy in those who commit unethical acts and the impact on victims, but the greater tragedy comes from those who can do something about it and choose to do nothing or rationalize a wrap on the knuckles.

It is for board attorneys who must defend allegations of wrong doing and yet still believe in fairness and justice, and not just winning.

This book is dedicated to the men and women of character and integrity and who take ethics seriously. It's dedicated to those who care.

*Honesty is the cornerstone of all success,
without which confidence and ability
to perform shall cease to exist.*

Mary Kay Ash

Table of Contents

About this Book	11
Major Themes	14
Executive Summary	17
Part 1. Ethics Merry Go-Wrong	21

    Major Points
    Ethics has a Human Face
    Reasons for Corporate and Personal Ethical Problems
    Get Back to Basics
    Ethics Defined

Part 2. Corporations & Nonprofits	34

    Major Points
    Capitalism with a Conscience
    Piercing the Organization Veil
    Lost Profit, Morale, and Productivity

Part 3. Sense of Self (SOS) Ethics without Social or Economic Status	48

    Major Points
    Humanness
    Let's Get Naked
    You're Dead – the Eulogy
    Success as a Human Being
    Sliding into the Moral Abyss
    Pay for the Lifestyle or Support Your Values
    Quiet Car
    Ethics and SOS Ethics is Simple
    HCF

Part 4. Develop Your Own SOS Ethics	86

    Things to Consider
    Golf & Ethics Go Together Like: Love and Marriage or a Horse and Carriage

Part 5. Building Blocks – Bringing It All Together	**101**
Appendix A	**104**
SOS Ethics Workbook	
Appendix B	**116**
Are You Living Ethically? Are You On the Right Path?	
Analysis	**120**
Bibliography	**124**
About the Author	**134**

It is not titles that honor men, but men that honor titles.

Niccolo Machiavelli

About this Book

1. This book carries with it no illusions. There always will be: good people who do unethical things; unethical people who get away with unethical behavior; and unethical people who know how to find and exploit loopholes and rationalize their behavior even if there is a policy or standards in place.

2. This book takes an approach all too often overlooked or not emphasized enough. Ethics must be personalized.

3. This book permits the overlap of personal and professional ethics. It encourages the mixing of the two. Although at times they are discussed separately, it is important to approach ethics from a combined personal-professional perspective.

4. Ethics, civic duty, social responsibility, and good corporate citizenship should be approached and thought of with a human face.

5. Corporate ethics goes well beyond social responsibility, such as going-green, environmental concerns, or not profiting from Third World sweatshops.

6. Ethics includes ordinary people that can least afford to be hurt by unethical or exploitive marketing strategies of a major corporation. Deception in marketing is a choice made by senior management that can financially hurt a family or individual. Unfair and hidden bank fees are an example. Unethical behavior can hurt others.

7. The book recommends that ethics, especially in MBA programs, start with how people interact with one another. It recommends how an absence of ethics takes a human toll. Ethics must have a human face if business leaders of today, and those of tomorrow, are to "take them to heart."

8. Ethics is flesh and blood. People develop marketing or internal policies, not faceless organizations, and they can directly impact staff, clients, or customers.

9. Ethical indiscretions are not victimless. Independent of the fines that can be paid is the human toll.

10. Ethics has less to do with character then many people realize. People of generally good character do bad things.

11. The book takes a radical departure from how ethics is taught and applied. Ethics often looks at liability, improper conduct, risk management, the actual or potential fines paid by a corporation, and the likely changes needed in law or policies to prevent a similar problem from occurring in the future.

12. The starting point for promulgating an ethics policy should not merely be liability or risk management. It must include a human component. What happens if people are hurt?

13. Ethical problems in business, government, and nonprofits are caused by a systematic failure to focus on human nature. Laws, rules, policies, regulations, or MBA classes will never fully address the crisis that exists unless analysis and understanding of human nature is included.

14. Ethics should never be discussed and analyzed in the abstract. Ethics should never be compartmentalized as it is today. Ethical compartmentalization is destructive. It is no longer linked to the wholeness of the individual. A person is expected and encouraged to wear different hats for different social and professional cultures. This is wrong.

15. Today's ethical problems have less to do with an absence of, or the failure to apply: laws, rules, and regulations and more to do with an individual's Sense of Self (SOS). This SOS can be lost for the short- or long-term. The loss for any period of time causes personal and professional problems. This speaks to the greater issue of not knowing ourselves. It speaks to spiritual wellness or as some described it – our authentic self.

16. Personal values of a manager, employee, business owner, or non-profit leader will shape and contribute to a workplace culture independent of any policies in place.

17. It is critical that every person routinely check-in with him- or herself quarterly or annually to ask why they're a successful person without citing degree(s), career, fine car, social status, or the image shown to the world.

18. The book can be used as a guide to enhance existing policies, or better train staff or board members. It also offers insights into self which makes it a personal self-improvement book as well.

19. The book is written for: MBA students, business owners, employment coaches, non-profit executives, frustrated professionals, ethics compliance officers, professionals at a career crossroads, and corporate and nonprofit board members.

20. Five parts make up this book: Ethics Merry Go-Wrong; Corporations & Nonprofits; Sense of Self (SOS) Ethics without Social or Economic Status; Develop Your Own SOS Ethics; and Building Blocks – Bringing It All Together.

21. Appendix A is a workbook to assist you in developing a Sense of Self (SOS) Ethics that brings together your values for Ethical Living.

22. Appendix B is a survey to help you and organizations to assess the ethical culture that impacts both.

Major Themes

You are ethics.

Ethics are not laws, policies, or regulations.

Ethics are people and interpersonal relationships.

Ethics has a human face. Ethics is a Sense of Self (SOS). Ethics is being a Successful Human Being. Ethics is Spiritual Health and Wellness.

Collectively, they are Ethical Living.

Ethical Living is the same for everyone. It does not matter if you're a taxicab driver or CEO of a large bank – ethics is ethics. Whether Wall Street or Main Street, ethics is universal.

Ethics, whether personnel policies or marketing strategies, are developed by and impact people. Ethics has a human face because directly or indirectly they always involve the interaction and relationship with people in a fair, respectful manner.

Core ethical values no matter the time or place don't change. If you carefully consider the many personal and organizational dramas that make the news you'll find there is a consistent element in each of them. People behave badly toward one another.

The quality, absence, or existence of policies, business strategies, or risk management protocols cannot determine human behavior. People draft them. People decide how to implement them. People are impacted by them whether staff, colleagues, consumers, or customers.

Core, universal ethical values are consciousness of one's personal humanity and the humanity of others. This consciousness is Sense of Self (SOS).

As noted earlier, together, the human face of ethics and having SOS Ethics is Ethical Living. Ethical Living is not a formula that must be consciously applied. It should come naturally like breathing and without difficulty.

Although I'm a lawyer, this book is not a legal analysis. Nor is it an academic endeavor. It is a practical examination that underscores the human perspective in ethics too often overlooked. As Founder of Entrepreneur Spirit (www.EntrepreneurSpirit.biz) and Corporate Chaplaincy (www.CorporateChaplaincy.biz) this is what I emphasize in working with organizations concerned about growing an ethical culture – encourage the personal integrity of staff. This is the Sense of Self that helps give ethics its human face.

I'm learning all the time.
The tombstone will be my diploma.

Eartha Kitt

Executive Summary

- Personalize ethics. Don't make ethics into an intellectual exercise or a cookie cutter formula to be applied. Put yourself in the place of the staff or customer who is likely to be impacted by a policy or marketing strategy. Imagine yourself on the receiving end.

- Ethics involves three distinct areas: breaking the law (embezzlement, insider trading, check fraud, running a red light, etc.); doing the right thing even if the law doesn't require it (treating difficult colleagues with dignity and respect at all times or not tricking clients or customers with gimmicks); and sometimes breaking the law if obeying it is unethical or immoral (violating segregation laws or hiding and protecting Jews during World War II).

- Ethics without a human face never will be firmly rooted and nurtured to grow in a social or organizational environment.

- Ethics is not only about exorbitant bonuses, negligent foreclosures, shady investments, accounting cover ups, or the ingenious ways someone found to circumvent the law. Ethics gone wrong have significant consequences to families and individuals. Good corporate citizenship goes beyond sponsoring community events.

- Many people can be hurt when ethics are breached. Children can be humiliated from a parent's professional indiscretion that becomes public. Risky corporate decisions can lose money hurting 401K accounts of retirees. Inept lawyering and paper shuffling by lazy employees can result in illegal or premature foreclosures.

- Young business leaders or students in MBA programs cannot empathize with faceless case studies.

- A company's ethics policy should complement the expectations employees have regarding fairness, right and wrong, and respect for clients, colleagues, and customers.

- Don't overthink ethics in personal or professional life. Laws, rules, policies, manuals, regulations, or marketing plans are secondary. They are always about people and how they're treated and how you want to be treated.

- Not keeping the focus on relationships contributes to the ethics crisis in business today. You don't have to like someone or even trust them to *respect their personhood*.

- Consider an ethics policy that includes the worst case scenario for a client or consumer. As one example, improper or negligent foreclosures are focused on statistics and the economic impact on a community after the fact. Rarely, do ethics begin with how the lives of families and individuals are, and could be changed. Lives can be ruined.

- Ethical indiscretions often have long-term consequences and individuals must be reminded of this reality.

- Each individual should develop their Sense of Self (SOS) Ethics that has a universal foundation. Live it. Review it. Be proud of it.

- Ethics cannot be expected if individuals have a flawed SOS Ethics.

- SOS Ethics is shaped by several things which include one's humanness. SOS Ethics enables the individual to be a better person, professional, and business leader.

- Teaching or understanding ethics as something impersonal is a mistake. Someone can be a wonderful spouse and parent, but still have questionable ethics because they have compartmentalized their life.

- Although there is clear overlap, being ethical and obeying the law should be understood separately as well as together.

- A person's SOS Ethics will directly impact revenue, productivity, and influence the ethical environment in every professional setting. If you think you have a strong SOS, then strip away your degree(s), career title, and social status of any kind to determine what's at your spiritual core. What makes you a man or woman? What makes you Tom, Maria, Peter, or Linda? This goes to a spiritual, not religious, element.

Man – a being in search of meaning.

Plato

1. Ethics Merry Go-Wrong

Major Points

- *Ethics is all or nothing.*

- Ethics requires vigilance. Organizational culture is set and nurtured at the top. You, as an individual, decide how to behave and react.

- A working definition of "ethics" is important before policies are written for the workplace. Staff and board members need to be working off the same basic definition of ethics.

- Ethics are universal regardless of your profession or the size of your organization. There are no gray areas if you have personal values and are not defined by poorly written policies or those that allow for shades of gray. Ethics is not gamesmanship. Nor are they amoral. Ethics is not rationalization and failing to take personal ownership.

- Would you be proud to tell your kids what you did at work today? Would you want them to emulate you? How does your behavior directly impact others?

- Spend more time on application and less time on creating long, cumbersome models that tend to over complicate issues. Problems often have simple core elements to their solution.

- Every ethical concern or conflict of interest whether personal or professional should be addressed with the same fundamental values.

- Don't lose track of the big picture.

- There are eleven basic elements that contribute to ethical lapses: (1) Depersonalization; (2) Interchanging ethics with legality; (3) Failing to take personal ownership; (4) Humility; (5) Check-ins with yourself; (6) Making ethics more complicated than they are;

(7) Unaddressed mental health issues; (8) Finding stillness; (9) Constant attention to application; (10) Forgetting to ask why; and (11) Failure to remember ethical lapses are not victimless.

Ethics has a Human Face

Don't lose focus on the big picture. It is always about how people are treated whether the motivation is liability, legal mandates, or employee and customer satisfaction.

Anxiety, suicide, depression, homelessness, delayed retirement, financial ruin, and family embarrassment are among the impacts for unethical behavior. The human toll is rarely considered in the business classroom. Despite the models, theories, and exhaustive efforts to dice, splice, and understand this esoteric word called "ethics" the global economy isn't better off.

In looking at the Wall Street meltdown, for example, the media was filled with stories about bonuses, weak regulatory oversight, calls for stronger oversight, hedge fund investing by banks, the incestuous marriage between subprime mortgages and variable-rate mortgages, and the complicity of the two major political parties in Washington that enabled risky banking practices. As a result, hundreds of thousands of financial services sector employees were laid off. It's easy to depersonalize this as merely a statistic forgetting the physical, emotional, and psychological impact unemployment has on these individuals and their families. Imagine being 55-years old when it happened with two kids in college?

Bill Moyers on his PBS program cited a *New York Times* article when discussing the financial services industry with a banking reform advocate. According to the piece cited, "As unemployment climbed and tax revenue fell the city of Baltimore laid off employees and cut services in the midst of the financial crisis. Its leaders now say the city's troubles were aggravated by bankers' manipulation of … [a] key interest rate linked to hundreds of millions of dollars the city had borrowed." This is one of many, many examples of the long-term consequences of weak ethics. Playing with interest rates isn't about inept business decisions. It's about losing a sense of direction individually and collectively as an organization.

Reasons for Corporate and Personal Ethical Problems

Despite the money spent on research, consultants, expensive and painfully boring 1,000-page books written for MBA students struggling with too much student loan debt, or the quickness of individuals to be gleeful at the crash and burn of another human being due to a moral misstep; the actual causes for ethical lapses still baffle those who do them and those who study the issue.

Identified below are eleven basic elements that directly impact ethics in the workplace or personal lives.

1. Depersonalization. Organizations are not monolithic beings with their own mind. Nothing happens or can happen without someone making a decision individually or collectively. Even an omission reflects a form of decision making, albeit a poor one. All too often people hide behind the corporate veil blaming the entity or the culture for actions made by individuals.

2. Ethics vs. legality. Separate the two. History teaches there were many laws like slavery, anti-Semitism, colonialism, and segregation that were unethical or immoral. People of

conscience broke these laws. Even today there are unjust laws and they remain "legal."

3. <u>Check-ins</u>. People forget to do this with themselves on an annual or quarterly basis. What have I become? Is it worth it? Contrary to the cliché, life isn't about dying with the most toys. Life is being true to self and understanding your value is not about status. How is your spiritual wellness? Do you think about your spiritual health as much as your mental or physical health?

4. <u>Personal Ownership</u>. Some ethics experts would say deciding between attending a daughter's sweet-sixteen birthday party or meeting with the company's high level managers from out of town is an ethical dilemma. It's not. There are some personal decisions, like this one, that should not be rationalized. Take ownership. These things will happen, but if they occur on an ongoing basis you need to do a check in at the end of the year and ask if it is worth it. Personal ownership also involves your role in a policy when the organization is later fined for it, but there are no consequences for you.

5. <u>Humility</u>. Again and again people make bad choices because they have deluded themselves into thinking they are smarter or better than others, and don't need feedback. The ancient gods forgave humankind for all of its sins, but one ... hubris.

6. <u>Overly complicated</u>. Ethics aren't complicated. Situations may get complicated, but the basic ethical principles and their application don't change. Truth can be uncomfortable, but the *truth is the truth*.

7. <u>Mental health</u>. Whether we realize it or not, much of our life is anchored in some level of mental health. Are we living someone else's expectations? Are we trying to prove our worth through a career to substitute something lacking in childhood like parental affirmation? Burying emotional pain can be projected or acted out in other ways like avoiding conflict, having passive-aggressive issues, bullying staff or colleagues, or feeling defeated

as a person will impact the workplace and others. Although mental health can have some overlap with spiritual wellbeing, they are distinct.

8. <u>Stillness</u>. Twitter, text messaging, twenty-four hour news cycles, twenty-four hour specialty channels like Sci-Fi, History, BBC America, or the Sports Network discourages us from reflecting more, finding the quiet to do it, or seeking the complete stillness to calm the mind, body, and soul to think about *nothing*. This speaks to spiritual health and wellness.

9. <u>Application</u>. There is disconnect between what we know is wrong, and how to apply those values. It is a bit like a college student doing all the course reading and expecting a multiple choice exam, instead getting an essay think-paper. The student must apply principles, not regurgitate information. Expecting people to follow an ethics model is the wrong approach. People need to apply principles, not models. Otherwise individuals are being inhibited from thinking through a problem. Legalism will trump logic and common sense.

10. <u>Ask Why</u>. "Why" is a great one word question, though it can get annoying. It is a powerful word that should prompt everyone on an ongoing basis. "Why did I just agree to something that makes me uncomfortable" "Why is this fair to our clients?"

11. <u>Consequences</u>. What is the impact for certain behavior to family, customers, etc.? What's the worst case scenario? Would I still think it is ethical if it were on the front page of the newspaper?

Get Back to Basics

Ethics is written about by experts, academics, business leaders, and even politicians throughout the world in books, magazines, and newspapers. There are even institutes on ethics. It is one of those words we hear a lot … but what does it actually mean? Consider the core principles of ethics.

Ethics Defined

Attempting to provide a definitional narrative about ethics is difficult. It is more useful to offer some observations about ethics and the elements that should be considered when understanding them.

- Ethics is people who see the necessity to respect and be respected.

- Ethics is a two way street. People write ethics policies and people are impacted by them. No one should be allowed to hide behind a workplace culture when something goes wrong. Nor should people, like consumers, who are negatively impacted become faceless statistics.

- Ethics impact employee behavior toward one another, and how clients or customers are treated.

- Ethics of every kind must have a similar foundation. Ethics need to have a universal nature that is the starting point in every personal and professional situation.

- Ethics needs to be directly linked to the best we are as individuals and to an organization's mission statement concerning goals and good corporate citizenship.

- Ethics cannot be compartmentalized between private and professional conduct.

- Ethics is legally and non-legally binding conduct. Ethics is not merely about liability or risk management, but also respect for staff and customers, fairness to staff and customers, openness and honesty to staff and customers, and truth shown to staff and customers.

Ethics has become rather complicated and over-intellectualized. Below is just a sample of "disciplines" or "specific types" of ethics that have entered the public arena for study and application. While it is an incomplete list, it reflects, in part, the lack of focus on the big picture and instead getting caught up in minutia or the "process" making the whole point of ethics lost.

Meta ethics
Legal ethics
Sexual ethics
Moral ethics
Kantian ethics
Societal ethics
Medical ethics
Analytic ethics
Personal ethics
Business ethics
Feminist ethics
Religious ethics
Humanist ethics
Naturalist ethics
Utilitarian ethics
Pragmatic ethics
Situational ethics
Existential ethics
Normative ethics
Marketing ethics
Axiological ethics
Descriptive ethics
Professional ethics
Postmodern ethics
Rationalistic ethics
Evolutionary ethics
Public service ethics
Deontological ethics
Consequential ethics
German idealistic ethics

There may be a need to explore the unique issues that arise in areas like lawyering or how a neighborhood responds to a drug rehab group moving in. Yet the human face of ethics is something overlooked or deemphasized, or even taken for granted within the formulas, discussions, or the policies that could be written with fewer pages. Shouldn't personal ethics involve honesty, integrity, and respect? How then are personal ethics different from sexual ethics? Whether it's legal, medical, or business ethics, or any other type shouldn't they all involve a foundation of respect, honesty, fairness, and communication, among other things?

Ethics should:

- Keep the individual and organization grounded.

- Provide the individual and organization perspective.

- Factor in the potential long-term consequences for weak ethics.

- Have the same set of standards and expectations for everyone in an organization.

- Keep the individual and the organization from doing something because everyone else is doing it. Two wrongs don't make a right even if it is an "industry standard" or "everyone else is doing it."

- Not be distinguished between personal and business. Why should there be one set of standards in the work place and another used in private life. Ethics is ethics. If allowances are made for things acceptable in one area that would not be normally acceptable in another, then trouble starts.

- *Trust is trust.* Trust shouldn't change in different situations. When something like trust and respect can't be depended on, then the individual(s) haven't recognized the human face of ethics. The human face of ethics reminds us our actions can directly impact others.

- Not merely include a company's contributions to a community or good causes. Otherwise, it implies that how profit or money is made is not important so long as there is substantial giveback to the community.

- Encourage the individual to draw on his or her values, not policies that are vague, incomplete, convoluted, or present opportunities to circumvent the rules.

Again, there may be a need to have disciplines within ethics, but no approach can begin without an appreciation for the dynamics of human nature and the hopes, desires, and insecurities that go with it. Every area of ethics cited above starts with a human face.

Rules and policies within organizations tell people what not to do in most cases. They can be highly punitive. Yet few express to people, other than going to jail or being fired, *why* certain things should not be done. *They don't invite people to have a conversation with themselves about right and wrong*, ethical and unethical.

Okay, so the chances of getting caught for helping the boss cook the books is very remote and you received an awesome, though undeserved bonus. *What if* you are caught by a savvy independent auditor? Suppose your name is listed in a newspaper, even if you are not accused of wrongdoing, just affiliated with the investigation? How will your eighty-year old father feel? Ethics is not about you alone.

Once a small ethical exception is made then it will lead to larger issues, and probably compromise an otherwise ethical culture.

Scott Thompson, Yahoo's short-lived CEO, took certain liberties on his resume. He never earned a computer science degree. It hasn't, however, limited Mr. Thompson's entrepreneurial prowess while at PayPal, Inovant LLP, Barclays Global Investors, and Coopers & Lybrand LLP. Because he has a demonstrated track record of success should it matter that he embellished his resume?

Yahoo's response to the controversy was clumsy and surprising. It described listing an unearned degree an "inadvertent error." Independent of the trust issues that may have arisen among staff, colleagues, and some board members, what does it say to the average worker? Are there different standards used? Is honesty and transparency only given lip service? If an employee sees wrongdoing in the work place should he or she keep quiet? If you perform well as an employee are there certain allowances for indiscretions?

In announcing the CEO's departure, the Yahoo press release was silent on the company's commitment to an honest, transparent culture. Although unintended, the impression was that Mr. Thompson's departure had less to do with misrepresentation, and more to do with negative publicity, and a shareholder's formidable proxy battle, if he stayed.

The press release did not contain any commitment by the Yahoo Board of Directors to a standard of conduct. It implied that falsity is okay if unnoticed. It's not just a matter of what was in the press release, but what wasn't. Yahoo is owed the benefit of the doubt. It is highly unlikely Yahoo's senior management intended to give this impression. Perhaps it's an innocent oversight.

Because Yahoo or any other organization gives to charity, helps the local community, or is a good corporate citizen, doesn't excuse a compromised internal culture or if profit is dependent on sweatshop labor. Corporate responsibility is internal and external.

A commitment to a healthy workplace culture starts at the top. The departure of a CEO due to a resume indiscretion is hardly a long-term problem for the company. Failing to identify, understand, and comprehensively address problematic cultural issues is the long-term concern. This commitment must stem from doing right for the sake of it, not because of lawsuits, proxy fights, or bad publicity. If an organization is committed to an ethical culture, which is set by senior management, then one set of rules applies to everyone. If a board of directors is committed to ethics it must be engaged with all levels of staff to have a sense of the larger culture in the organization.

To err is human, but it feels divine.

Mae West

2. Corporations & Nonprofits

Major Points

- Conduct an Ethics Audit annually. This should include anonymous staff surveys to garner a sense of the organization's culture. Surveys should be handled by a board member or committee with results shared with the whole board.

- If the organization is large enough consider an anonymous hotline.

- Staff is an extension of an organization's image and reputation. Employees should be proud of their work place and the organization's values. If they're not, it is a warning sign.

- It's easy to overlook an ethical issue. As noted earlier, a law or policy need not be violated for an ethical issue to arise. Staff bullying, for example, is often tolerated. Organizationally, people need to be aware and trained concerning the emergence of ethical matters which include, for example, office bullying.

- Don't let your office or organization become rich material for a Dilbert comic strip. Focus on results in an ethical manner, and not process.

- If people must be constantly managed, ask why they're not motivated. How can they be motivated?

- Ethics classes need to be ongoing and workshops offered no less than once a year. Participants should include staff and board representation to underscore the seriousness of ethics in the workplace.

- The board of directors as a whole should also receive regular training.

- Ethics Officers or Compliance Officers need to answer directly to the board or a subcommittee of its members.

- "Lying, deception, and omissions of key facts in this agreement are illegal and unethical. Such conduct may result in job loss, needless litigation, criminal prosecution, ruined professional reputation, and public embarrassment to family and friends." These sentences or something similar to them merit starting every contract. It forces the signers, and those who have drafted the document, not to overlook the obvious and to underscore upfront the personal and organizational consequences for failing to behave in a legal and ethical manner (See Joffe-Walt and Spiegel).

Capitalism with a Conscience

Comedian George Carlin quipped, as have many others since, "business ethics" are an oxymoron. Although the two words are understood as a contradiction, to some a business or non-profit can be managed in an ethical manner, if the people in management bring certain values to the table. In one sense, there is no such thing as "business ethics." There should not be a set of values children are raised with, and another expected later in professional life.

It is troubling to hear an organization boast about doing the right thing. You get rewarded for doing the right thing as if a pedestrian should be grateful when a driver stops at a crosswalk to obey the law. Let me modify the Golden Rule – do onto others as you would want done onto you and your family.

If someone were a manager of a chemical factory with schools and neighborhoods not far away, all the person needs to do is ask "what if my children were hurt by an environmental policy my team set?"

Business schools need to teach the *personalization of ethics*. Otherwise, it is more likely than not the individual acting alone or on a team won't take personal responsibility for something that goes wrong, but rather hide behind the organization veil, especially after legal counsel signed off.

Those in positions of authority must condition themselves to ask whether they'd be comfortable with the policy if a family member or close friend were impacted by it.

It is absurd to think that capitalism can, or should, have a conscience. Capitalism is an economic system to which individuals bring values, principles, and perspectives. People need to have a conscience and not hide behind a corporate face or economic structure. It is equally absurd, or at the very least very troubling, when some business schools try to teach or develop ethical behaviors or in one case train "just and humane leaders."

It still baffles me that tomorrow's business executives need to be taught about justice and humanity. Are parents failing if their college age children need to be trained to be "just and humane?" Granted, not all parents may be ideal. Or no matter the best parental efforts, Junior may turn out to be a rotten apple.

According to new research, "The vast majority of us ... are capable of behaving in profoundly unethical ways" (Joffe-Walt and Spiegel). This has the potential to include you and me. I hope it is a fair conclusion that the vast majority of us try to do the right thing, but we are all capable of wandering off the straight and narrow. As Mae West once remarked, "I use to be as pure as Snow White, but I drifted."

It seems business education, in some cases, seeks to divide the person, rather than finding the commonality of values and principles that bring the person together as a single being with his or her profession. Students should never forget that as professionals and business leaders their decisions have consequences.

Prof. Luigi Zingales identified in a Bloomberg article what may be the central problem to ethics today. It's not merely a corrupt organizational culture, or a candidate selection process which devalues ethics that contributes to today's problems, but the quality of education business students receive.

In his piece, *Do Business Schools Incubate Criminals?*, Prof. Zingales observed that the education most students receive, discuss situations where ethics arise without offering clear right or wrong answers. Instead, the student has discretion in approaching the resolution to the case study. As the professor suggests there should be no room in most cases for dealing with ethical matters. He further noted another problem in business education is the individual need not take ownership for his or her behavior because of the emphasis on the organization. The person can hide behind the faceless corporation.

In addition to the very important points made in Prof. Zingales' article, ethics should also be taught in junior high, reinforced in high school, and further underscored in college and graduate school. There are universal values that transfer to any job, organization, social setting, or in any part of an individual's life.

Piercing the Organization Veil

Merely fining a company deflects accountability. Miraculously, it is the organization's fault or its culture that accounts for ethical lapses. For-profit and nonprofit entities are not possessed with a mind of their own. Functioning entities cannot act without the direction of puppeteers. In addition, sometimes it is more profitable for an organization to do the wrong thing and pay a fine. It becomes even more important to focus on all the individuals involved in the decision making process. People make decisions, not organizations.

Although a bank, corporation, or other entity including a non-profit does something egregious, few individuals lose their jobs, go to jail, or get publicly reprimanded. State or federal governments are quick to settle out of court when entities agree to pay large fines. Buried beneath the headlines and the dollar figures is one underreported, if not overlooked, important fact – the lack of personal ethics and individual responsibility. As noted earlier people set, manipulate, or ignore the policies that cause businesses, corporations, or nonprofits problems.

Robert F. Bruner, Dean of the Darden Business School at the University of Virginia, referred to the "humanistic perspective of business" during an interview. He underscored "human obligations" and the "humility of decision-making."

Goldman Sachs has been around for almost a century and a half. Yet there are critics of how it does business. Time has not ironed out the ethical wrinkles. It's another example a commitment to ethics must be constant and carried on by every new generation of professional or business executive.

A March 2012 op-ed in the *New York Times* highlighted one of those wrinkles. A mid-level manager making a six figure salary resigned after almost 12 years in the company citing Goldman Sachs lost its sense of "teamwork, integrity, a spirit of humility, and always doing right by our clients." He added it made him ill "how callously people talk about ripping their clients off. Over the last 12 months I have seen five different managing directors refer to their own clients as 'muppets'…"

It's hard to believe Goldman Sachs didn't have an ethics infrastructure in place. Did senior management merely give it lip service? Any policies in place can't act or be applied by themselves. They are nothing more than tools or guides waiting for someone competent and deft in the corporate environment to review, update, and apply. Put another way, it's like owning a car, but you choose to hitch hike instead. Nothing is worth its salt unless it is understood and properly used.

If the allegations made by the former mid-level manager are accurate, the question becomes about those responsible for keeping an eye on the culture. Was there disconnect between the pressures of meeting profit goals and maintaining standards that didn't treat clients like muppets?

What happened, if anything to client respect, trust placed in individual brokers, and more important the personal integrity of the brokers who may have referred to clients as muppets? Would they want a parent, grandparent, or best friend treated as a muppet?

Perhaps a disturbing example of it relates to a decision made by the U.S. Department of Justice (DOJ). In August 2012, DOJ determined it lacked sufficient evidence to criminally prosecute anyone at Goldman Sachs. DOJ reached its decision despite the findings of the U.S. Senate Permanent Subcommittee on Investigations which documented wrongdoing in a massive investigative bipartisan report released in April 2011.

"Our investigation of the origins of the financial crisis revealed wrongdoing and failures among mortgage lenders, banking regulators, credit rating agencies and investment banks," commented Sen. Carl Levin, Chair of the Subcommittee, in a statement after learning the news. "One of those investment banks, Goldman Sachs, created complex securities that included "junk" from its own inventory that it wanted to get rid of. It misled investors by claiming its interests in those securities were "aligned" with theirs while at the same time it was betting heavily against those same securities, and therefore against its own clients, to its own substantial profit. Its actions did immense harm to its clients, and ***helped create the financial crisis that nearly plunged us into a second Great Depression***" (emphasis added).

Lost jobs, mortgage foreclosures, depleted 401K accounts, investment portfolio devaluations, and difficulty finding employment at the same pay scale, among other things have impacted millions of people. These are not faceless statistics. The anxiety, depression, and emotional trauma this has caused cannot be calculated with numbers. It's another example that *ethical lapses have significant consequences even if no law is technically violated.*

Lawyers who often write ethics policies tend to focus on liability and risk management. Hence, sometimes policies lack the balance to do what's right though there is no legal mandate. Arrogance, for example, is not illegal. Calling clients muppets isn't illegal. Hubris, however, can undercut an organization's reputation, and potentially lead to inappropriate conduct.

Several years ago, then New York Attorney General Andrew Cuomo announced a settlement with Bank of America. The institution agreed to "return over $4.5 billion to investors across New York State and the nation." According to the Attorney General's office, "These agreements settle allegations that Bank of America and RBC [Royal Bank of Canada] made misrepresentations in its marketing and sales of auction-rate securities. Bank of America and RBC marketed and sold auction-rate securities as safe, cash-equivalent products, when in fact they faced increasing liquidity risk."

Who determined to make these misrepresentations? Who signed off on them? Let's cut to the chase and lose the nice word "misrepresentation" and call it for what it is – who lied to consumers? Someone, or several people, decided to lie to boost revenue and no doubt secure huge end of the year bonuses. Who are these individuals? What were the consequences for them? Weren't there lawyers to tell them "misrepresentations" are illegal? Did lawyers sign off on this marketing strategy?

Did the people who conceived these "misrepresentations" exchange personal ethics for corporate ethics? Shouldn't there be some similarities between the two? Were their personal ethics different from professional ethics? Would these same bankers have pushed these "auction-rate securities" on grandparents with a fixed income or people they loved?

This seems to be a large part of the problem today. The individuals responsible for this mess no doubt still see themselves as good, decent people. Yet there is one set of rules for work and another for life outside of business. They may be exceptional spouses or parents and yet don't seem to think twice about crafting policies that eventually led to a whopping $4.5 billion mistake.

In 2011, New York Attorney General Eric T. Schneiderman announced a "$58.75 million settlement with Wachovia Bank N.A. and Wells Fargo Bank, N.A., as its successor, as part of an ongoing national investigation of alleged anticompetitive and fraudulent conduct in the municipal bond derivatives industry."

Independent of internal controls or the failure to apply an ethics policy – how can any of this occur without an individual or individuals signing off on this "fraudulent conduct." There was a civil fine, but no criminal penalty. Someone or several people do something wrong and in many cases watch the organization's money make the problem go away.

Similar to the example cited before what were the lawyers doing? Forget the Code of Ethics the legal profession has for itself. It is confusing why lawyers are so infrequently taken to task when there is a scandal. Lawyers review most organizational policies, procedures, and other documents. Are they not aware of what's happening? Why? There can be no useful case studies until we actually know who knew what, and when, and what they did, or didn't do with the information.

There are no real consequences for many individuals who played a role in "fraudulent conduct" because they are able to justify, rationalize, or hide behind the organizational veil and culture. Cultures are created by people. They don't just happen. What happened to a personal sense of fairness or right and wrong? This is why Sense of Self Ethics is so important.

Some would argue the expectations in the work place are different. Perhaps. But ask yourself this – if you were an employee or senior manager to one of the above banks would you want to be on the receiving end of what Wachovia, Wells Fargo or Bank of America did? If the answer is no, and it's fair to say probably everyone would say no, how can those setting these policies do so with a clear conscience?

In 2012, findings by the National Business Ethics Survey found approximately 62 million Americans or 45% admitted to having seen ethical violations. Even if the statistic was 10% it would be troubling. If

43

the organizations of those surveyed were evaluated there would be a commonality to all of the violations and they could be grouped into the same set of categories.

Independent of an organization's daily management there is the issue of board members who are disengaged. One of the greatest disservices a non-profit or corporate board can do to an organization and its staff is to be totally dependent on senior management for its information or to allow information from lower management to be shaded or manipulated by senior officials. The crash and burn of so many CEOs in recent years should underscore that boards need to be more active. Ethics officers and risk managers, for example, need to meet with board members privately or with subcommittees without the presence of senior management.

Just because numbers look good doesn't mean there aren't problems. Staff can do a sterling job not because of senior management, but in spite of it. There are instances where committed professionals do the best job they can because they believe in excellence and professionalism. They do so while managing abusive supervisors, absentee bosses, or controlling bosses that make the simple complicated and the work environment unpleasant.

This also applies to business owners or senior executives in very large companies who rely on others to inform them of what's going on in the frontlines. The value of it can't be any clearer than "Undercover Boss" on CBS. Business owners and corporate executives disguise themselves to look like new employees. They see firsthand some of the challenges of staff and the business. It's an opportunity to get pure data that hasn't been altered, massaged, and/or packaged to please the owner.

The most important thing to remember is an organization cannot do anything without the direct, active involvement of people who determine the tone and culture of ethics in the workplace. Organizations are never to blame for something that goes wrong. Otherwise, it would be comparable to blaming "cars" for accidents and fining the dealership or manufacturer rather than holding individual drivers accountable.

Lost Profit, Morale, and Productivity

The fines paid by corporations for ethical lapses are staggering. They annually exceed billions of dollars. On a smaller scale failing to address or provide provisions in ethics policies for abusive bosses, as one example, destroys morale and productivity. Don't expect staff to go above and beyond the call of duty if no action is taken against the office bully. You can further expect sick time to be maximized. Even small nonprofits can develop a reputation in a community for being "a place you don't want to work."

Healthy ethics cultures create trust between staff and management. It furthers team cohesion. A positive and deserved reputation is earned in the community as place worthy of time and talent. Professional satisfaction increases and can be sustained. Ethics is proactive and can anticipate litigation or regulatory fines. They underscore employees are not alone when making tough decisions and the organization will back them up. Good ethics saves and makes organizations money while showing staff and customers the respect and fairness they deserve.

In developing internal (personnel) and external (marketing) ethics policies, don't assume this responsibility should fall to a lawyer or human resources personnel. Lawyers are trained to keep things legal. An organization can be doing everything legal, but the perception is that it is unethical. Think about the Goldman Sachs example cited earlier. It's not necessarily the job of a lawyer to look at policies from an ethical prism. They keep organizations out of *legal* trouble.

Similarly, human resources personnel are trained to draft or apply policies in a manner that may not always consider short- or long-term ethical issues. Personnel knowledge is not the same as ethics expertise. If an organization is too small to a have a full-time ethics officer then one should be kept on retainer for staff, counsel, the board, or human resources to consult.

Why was man created on the last day? So that he can be told, when pride possesses him:
God created the gnat before thee.

The Talmud

3. Sense of Self (SOS) Ethics without Social or Economic Status

Major Points

- Develop and use every day your own Sense of Self (SOS) Ethics in everything *you* do – work and play.

- Write a short ethics statement for *yourself*. It should apply to your personal and professional life.

- Don't take your values for granted. Think about them. Do you apply them to all parts of your life? Are you one person at the office and someone else at home?

- How successful you are as a human being will shape and nurture your SOS Ethics.

- It might seem like an odd question to ask, but are you a successful human being? Why? It has nothing to do with financial or professional success. Are the persons at Goldman Sachs who referred to customers who trusted them as "muppets" successful human beings? Is there room for improvement?

- Awareness, perspective, conscience, and consciousness are among the elements to better understand, develop, and use SOS Ethics.

- If you were socially, educationally, and professionally naked who are you?

- At your eulogy what would you like people to say and remember most about you? Does this square with both your professional and private life? Do you have different standards for different situations?

48

Carl Rogers, a humanistic-psychologist, wrote people are a product of their environments. There is a reason we do what we do, whether it is grow personally and professionally or crash and burn. Rogers observed there is some kind of inner call, a longing to "self-actualize." Self-actualize can be defined as being true to one's creation. In order to be true to one's self the individual must fully realize his or her "human-beingness." *Behavior and Sense of Self (SOS) become one.*

I agree in part with Dr. Rogers. There are certain realities that influence behavior. A work environment that gives lip service to a personnel policy is one of them. A dangerous go-along-get-along mentality may take hold. Mediocre staff may become the senior manager's favorites enabling them to take certain liberties at the expense of competent, hardworking staff. This contributes to a toxic work environment.

There is something inherent in our being that wants to be valued and wanted. Hence, humility, character, self-esteem, and personal dignity, among other things all play a factor in our success as a human being. It influences our personal and professional lives.

Humanness

Before you can have ethics, values, or principles you need to be conscious of your humanness in the purest, most basic form. You must have empathy for the consequences that an ethics violation may cause. The values of a successful human being carry over to everything done in life. I would describe this as a "spiritual element."

Don't roll your eyes thinking you've come upon a New Age book. Keep reading. Spiritual has nothing to do with dancing naked and howling at the moon, burning transcendental incense made at a granola shop in California, or fearing a cantankerous deity throwing lightning bolts.

Everyone is spiritual at some level. It doesn't matter if you're without belief in a higher power, not sure about it, or believe in it heart and soul. If you have ever been awed driving through mountains, seeing the surf at the seashore, holding your child or grandchild for the first time, enjoying a steaming mug of coffee on the deck watching the sun rise, or sitting silently in the park during the height of the autumn tapestry of color, you have had a kind of spiritual experience. It can be a moment or two when time seems suspended, life's pressures aren't a companion, and you want to be alive because of the way you feel at the moment. It is spiritual. It is a deeper Sense of Self.

Spiritual can take you to a simple, uncomplicated place. It takes away all the nonsense of life. Obviously, spiritual doesn't lend itself to easy definition. It can be a lot more complicated with many nuances, but hopefully you get the idea.

Spirituality is bound together with conscience and consciousness. Although conscience and consciousness are distinct, they are complementary. Together they can form a very powerful self-awareness. Sometimes it is an unwanted self-awareness, but it is still a powerful means of self-empowerment to see yourself, your place in the world, and your interactions with family, friends, colleagues, and romantic interests, from a different perspective.

This greater self-awareness lends itself to a growing trend in large organizations that now use "Corporate Chaplains." Employees and senior management are provided a non-judgmental advisor, guide, and listener to both workplace and private matters. A Corporate Chaplain is not someone who dispenses religious counseling per se, but rather tries to help the individual feel whole or complete and not compartmentalized. Sometimes an individual, even if successful, can feel uncertain in their private and professional lives. A Corporate Chaplain can help the individual frame the right questions about his or her life and career.

Spirituality in the broadest sense speaks to success as a human being. This contributes to behaviors and perceptions in private and professional life. This impacts ethics in and out of the workplace. It provides a spiritual awareness focused on personhood that has nothing to do with social, educational, or professional achievements of self and others.

Let's Get Naked

Think of yourself naked. You're not looking in the mirror. So there's no need to be self-conscious about your tuckus, love handles, or the nearby exercise equipment that's used as a clothes rack.

In the most basic sense who are you? There's no yummy figure, impressive steel pecks, wash board abs, car to show off, fancy watches or gold jewelry for a fashion statement, or clothes to make the man or woman to suggest an impressive career.

Have you ever been unemployed or even underemployed? It's awful isn't it? Anxiety, pressure, or calls from the bank about the mortgage can be part of this horrendous experience. One of the things I have noticed about many friends and colleagues who have been unemployed is how they sometimes allow themselves to be defined by a job. Independent of financial worries that keep them up at night, there are self-esteem issues.

Why do people feel lost? Again – this is not about the unbearable times that can be fixed by money. It is about who you are without the job. Sometimes we allow professional identity to get confused or incorporated with financial concerns and don't realize it. Unfortunately, we have allowed society to condition us to be defined by titles, career, etc. It's very easy to do. I still have concerns that I do it. Depending on the social setting the next time you're asked what you do, tell the individual you're an area distributor of bathroom urinal cakes to cleaning companies.

Who am I without a job? How much of my worry stems from a life style or public image that I seek to maintain? How much of it is legitimate worry about life's basics. The necessities of life are very elemental. Having experienced unemployment and career change I have been very fortunate that I have never identified or allowed myself to be defined by a job. Like everyone else in that situation, I have experienced stress and anxiety, but I never felt valueless or useless due to unemployment or not having a fancy title. I have been ambivalent about what to do next, where to look, whether I should move, etc., but never did I go into a kind of funk because I've lost my identity. A job did not define my personhood.

If individuals understood who they were as human beings, there would be fewer ethics problems in society today. If you don't have a sense of self, send out an SOS for help! Celebrities, politicians, and senior executives make the news daily for some level of indiscretion. None of this suggests that you are going to make the same mistakes, but it should give everyone pause to ask why people do certain things. If you put it in context, all of us are capable of making a life-changing mistake. We can learn a lot about human nature, and ourselves, by the unfortunate missteps of others. Don't take the slightest satisfaction in them, but be humble and ask whether there is even the chance you could screw up in the same way. Before you judge ask if you're any better?

There are laws, rules, regulations, social constructs, societal expectations, and codes of professional conduct. And still folks find ways to get into heaps of trouble. The writer Dostoevsky reflected in a letter to his brother during the first half of the Nineteenth Century that humankind "is a mystery: if you spend your entire life trying to puzzle it out, then do not say that you have wasted your time. I occupy myself with this mystery because I want to be a man." Put another way Dostoevsky wanted to understand what it meant to be a successful human being.

You can't determine if you're a successful human being *unless* you do a bit of soul searching. Take it all away! Take it all off! What makes you a good spouse, a good parent, a good colleague, a good manager, or a good neighbor? None of this has to do with money, education, or social status. If you miss your child's school plays or soccer games often, what does it matter if he or she has a television in the room, goes to a private school, or gets to wear designer clothes? It means little.

If you don't lose your Sense of Self you'll be a better person, leader, friend, spouse, and professional.

A Sense of Self should be an ongoing reality check. It keeps you humble. A Sense of Self reminds you there is always someone smarter, brighter, better educated, and more successful than you. And there is always someone smarter, brighter, better educated, and more successful than that person. So, don't be insecure about it. This is not to marginalize hard work for what anyone rightly and fairly earned. It's just a reality check. It should force everyone to think about what's ultimately important.

If you believe in a higher power, the maker of the universe isn't going to be impressed by any degree, success, or achievement. The maker of the stars, planets, mountains, etc., the grand designer of the heavens will not care or be impressed if you're a Pulitzer Prize winning author or a

Publishers Clearing House Winner. If you think we all end up as fertilizer and nothing more then you'll be the guest of honor at the ugly-bug ball.

Imagine if Members of Congress had a better Sense of Self. They'd remember power, their power, is built on shifting sand. In all likelihood, history will not remember most Congressmen and women. Some may get a park or federal building named after them, but how many people will know why, or even care after several years.

Many do what it takes to get re-elected, rather than do things that may get them booted even if in the long-run it's not good for America. In some cases it is nothing more than a need for attention. Who are they without being a Member of Congress? Yes, power does intoxicate and it does corrupt, yet there is a lot more going on. This isn't to suggest that there aren't many hard working men and women in Congress trying to do right by the American people. There are, however, many who feed on the attention, the limelight, and being courted because of their fleeting power.

If you watch PBS, look at the credits in the beginning of the show, documentary, or educational series. There are many foundations named after philanthropists no longer living. Do you know anything about their lives? Do you care? Will you take the time to find out? In New York City there is a convention hall named after one of the State's great citizens. It's called the Javits Center named for Jacob Javits. How many people even remember he was a distinguished U.S. Senator? With the passage of time even fewer will remember anything about him.

You're probably familiar with the scriptural passage, "For everything there is a season, and a time for every matter under heaven: a time to be born, and a time to die; a time to plant ..." (Ecclesiastes 3:1-3). It's often used during a funeral or sermon. Or you'll also recognize it from the song "Turn! Turn! Turn!" by The Byrds.

If you want a real downer read the whole chapter of Ecclesiastes in the Hebrew Scriptures (Old Testament). Regardless of your faith, religion, or spirituality consider reading it. A downer might be an exaggeration. It may give you a different outlook on life than the one you have now. It provides a well of insights and perspectives.

"Vanity of vanities ... All is vanity. What do people gain from all the toil at which they toil under the sun? A generation goes, and a generation comes ... The people of long ago are not remembered, nor will there be any remembrance of people yet to come by those who come after them (Ecclesiastes 1:1-4 & 11)." Now I have Dionne Warwick singing *What's it All About, Alfie?* in my head – "What's it all about, Alfie? Is it just for the moment we live? What's it all about when you sort it out, Alfie?"

Keep perspective. Try to stay humble. Stay focused on a higher power, or the infinite cosmos, not keeping up with appearances.

You're Dead – the Eulogy

Don't lose a sense of the big picture. What will folks read in your obituary some day? What will be your personal reputation at your time of death? What will a son, daughter, niece, or nephew say in a eulogy? We're conditioned to win, to succeed, to beat the other person whether by the rules or those we bend or break when no one is looking. Sometimes we live someone else's expectations which can be especially destructive.

Believe it or not your last breath, the ultimate last bow might be the biggest day of your life. It all comes together for critique, reflection, and celebration (in most cases) of those you leave behind. Who will speak, and what will be said at the eulogy? It's being naked in a very different kind of way. You can't change the wardrobe, trade in the car, or bark orders to staff to get something done. What will those who contributed to the financial meltdown which hurt millions of families and individuals think about at the end of their life?

Have you ever visited the graves of a famous person? I've visited several including Chopin, Edith Piaf, Eleanor Roosevelt, and Franklin D. Roosevelt. There they were – members of Death's Equalizer Club. Eleanor and Franklin changed the world. You may not agree with their politics, but they had a profound impact. There they rested in a simple garden near their Hyde Park home. There were no security guards around the President. Nor was the First Lady's scheduler deciding whether you get access. There were no tickets to buy for a Piaf or Chopin concert. Regardless of your faith – believer, non-believer, nature worshiper, or devotee of Jimmy Hendricks – we all end up in the same place. Whether there is a soul that goes on to a higher spiritual level is a different matter.

Leo Tolstoy focused on the quality of life's achievements, not the number or size. There is a beautiful passage in his short-story *Walk in the Light While there is Light*. "You say you would do twice, ten times, a hundred times, more than you did. But if you did ten thousand times ten thousand more than all men have done, what would that have been in the work of God? A mere nothing! God's work ... is infinite." Your work, your efforts, your volunteerism is "neither small nor great, it [is] God's work."

It doesn't matter your religious beliefs. If you're uncomfortable with the word "God" then substitute it with Goddess, Maker of the Universe, or a humanist or generic reference to something bigger than yourself. The above passage has something to offer everyone when thinking about developing and living by SOS Ethics.

Success as a Human Being

It shouldn't be strange to ask yourself – "Am I a successful human being?" In fact, it's a good idea to do it from time to time. Am I a successful human being toward colleagues? Am I a successful human being when it comes to customers or clients I represent? If you think it is silly, is it because the question is too difficult or it may make you uncomfortable. Or you've never given it much thought.

It might be one of the most important *and overlooked questions* in an individual's personal and professional life. If you answered "well duh, yeah I am a successful human being," provide a detailed explanation. What does it mean to be a successful human being? What makes you one? Your answer may surprise you.

If you're struggling to answer the question of what it means to be a successful human being, then you just had a life changing epiphany. Everyone should struggle with this question and it should be an ongoing discussion in your mind. Make it part of your daily journey.

Ask yourself what it means to be "Bill," "Sarah," "Justin," "Deb," "Dan," "Cindy," etc., without thinking about your job, religion, or education, or ethnic pride (i.e. Irish wit, Italian lover, etc.)?

I have a dear friend who often introduces me by saying "this is my good friend Paul and he does …" this, that, and the other thing. What if I'm just introduced as "this is my good friend Paul"? What does it mean to be "just" Paul? What does it mean just to be you?

One time I asked a candidate for governor in New Hampshire during an interview what he hoped God would say to him when called home. Professionally, he had done very well. He was wealthy, successful, and was courted to serve on high profile boards. Privately and personally he had a mixed reputation, especially in how he treated people. His mood soured, his body language changed, and he became quite uncomfortable in grasping for an answer. I wasn't trying to embarrass the man. I simply wanted to know what was under the flash, self-confidence, and no-nonsense business acumen. I wanted to know, what made him human. I wanted to know his core values.

In another case, while interviewing a U.S. Senator, I asked the Senator the same question about what God might say to her. Without missing a beat the Senator said, "Well done, good and faithful servant." This Senator by the way always introduces any staff person who accompanies her to events. She's also quick to say that part of her success as a lawmaker stems from having a hardworking, talented staff.

Several years ago business brought me to lower Manhattan. It was a crisp, sunny, refreshing autumn day. Linda, a middle aged homeless woman with white hair, soiled hands and feet, sat on a mat with her orange cat named Mary. Linda had a paper cup on the corner of the mat for donations, though she did not solicit them. I bent down, introduced myself, and petted Mary who purred in a joyous, welcoming way. I put $20 in Linda's cup. She looked at me with all sincerity and thanked me profusely. Then she added, "But will you have enough for yourself?"

Here's a woman who had nothing. Yet she had ethics, values, compassion. Though life had beaten her up she maintained a strong sense of self. She never lost her humanness. She never lost her humanity. Without question Linda was a successful human being. She could have taught those who call customers "muppets" a thing or two.

I still think about Linda and Mary. I still can see them sitting on the street as if it were yesterday. That empathetic, compassionate question, "But will you have enough for yourself?" will live with me forever. Her values showed recognition of someone else's personhood. Her conduct reflected ethics with a human face in more ways than one.

The Ukrainian philosopher and theologian Hryhorri Savych Skovoroda quipped, "God made everything necessary easy and everything unnecessary difficult." This isn't to suggest a person shouldn't have lofty goals. It does suggest we shouldn't lose sight of the basics in life. It's okay to have wealth, though it shouldn't become your reason to live. It's okay to have authority, but don't let it be used to control. It's okay to earn a title like doctor, lawyer, or candle stick maker, but don't forget it doesn't make you more important as a human being than someone else. Once someone loses sight of the basics, he or she has lost SOS Ethics and can be in personal and professional jeopardy.

Several years ago in January I had to evacuate my building as a snow storm arrived. An ominous fire across the parking lot had every indication of shooting sparks and flying debris onto my building.

"What should I take," I asked. I had no furry-four legged children to worry about. "Perhaps take the embroidery my grandmother made that hung framed on the wall? Maybe pack some of my music collection? What about my degrees?" I parked my car in an enclosed garage blocks away due to the storm. Without the car to load I didn't have many options.

Perhaps for the last time I surveyed my apartment. Before closing the door I looked at the many things that brought me comfort and pleasure – books, framed art, family photos, and autographed opera and ballet memorabilia.

For practical reasons I took my laptop, cell phone, brief case, and the clothes on my back. I took nothing else. I did forget my reading glasses which later annoyed the hell out of me.

I am not and will not be defined by "things." Although my grandmother's embroidery and many photos could not be replaced, people you love are held in the heart. Opera and ballet memorabilia is something in time and does not reflect what they are – a living, vibrant, dynamic feast for the eyes and ears. This kind of art lives in the moment. Clothes, books, framed reproductions of paintings, among other things can be replaced.

Before finally leaving the building I checked to make sure everyone was okay. Although my neighbors clearly were, gruff, testosterone-enthused police arrived to state the obvious. "You have to leave!"

Other than damage to some cars in the back lot and smoked-kielbasa aroma permeating the building our respective homes were fine the next day. Most important no pet or person was hurt.

If my soul or how the world perceives me is not defined by degrees, titles, my resume, or social status (or lack thereof) then by what? The answer is in my personhood and those of others.

Sliding into the Moral Abyss

Weston Smith, a former senior executive at Healthsouth Corporation told students at Mississippi State University's Richard C. Adkerson School of Accountancy that "being rich was fun, but I promise you, I have more joy in my heart today, living an honest life." Mr. Smith was a whistleblower who despite coming clean still did fourteen months in federal prison for his participation in a multi-billion dollar fraud.

As reported by the University's magazine, Mr. Adkerson underscored that small compromises grow into bigger ones. Individuals tend to feel a need to belong. They don't want to be seen as someone who isn't a team player. He suggested that each small compromise builds momentum and before the individual realizes it he or she has become part of the problem.

He advised students to constantly challenge themselves. He asked a very tough, thought-provoking question, "Are you strong enough in your belief system to walk away from it?"

Let me add to Mr. Adkerson's point about losing a Sense of Self. In addition to having the courage to walk away from it, are you willing to be fired for not being a "team player"? You're an employee at will – you can be fired for no reason. Your position can be eliminated and job functions divided up into several existing positions. What is your exit strategy from a job where lip service is given to ethics that impact staff and customers?

One of New York City's greatest mayors, Fiorello H. LaGuardia (yes, for whom the airport in New York City is named), cautioned when it came to doing what's right, when it came to ethics, when it came to being true to self and serving the greater good – if you have to think about it – "You're a goner."

There are other factors that can play a role in losing a Sense of Self. Here's an extreme situation. Former New York Governor Eliot Spitzer resigned because of a prostitution scandal. Spitzer had served as State Attorney General before getting elected to the top office by a landslide. As Attorney General he was nicknamed the "Sheriff of Wall Street" for taking on what he alleged were unscrupulous companies. He arrived in the Governor's Office pledging to clean up Albany from incestuous, status-quo politics where transparency and accountability is as popular as garlic to a vampire, silver bullets to a werewolf, or Ethel Merman belting out show tunes that could scare off zombies.

As the Capitol of New York, Albany is a jaded town. There isn't much it hasn't seen before. But jaws dropped when the prostitution scandal broke involving the "Sheriff of Wall Street," Governor Eliot Spitzer. His supporters were demoralized and devastated. Critics gleefully danced like cats on the hot tin roof of a fish cannery.

Through it all, however, not one person asked, what would drive such an extraordinarily bright guy to risk and throw it all away, including a beautiful family, by patronizing high priced prostitutes? Fraud and hypocrite were among the more charitable descriptions given to Gov.

64

Spitzer. Dig a little deeper. It's not about being a fraud or hypocrite. I sincerely believe that Gov. Spitzer was neither a fraud nor hypocrite.

In 2010, *Client 9: The Rise and Fall of Eliot Spitzer*, was released. Most gave the movie rave reviews. It included interviews with Spitzer, his enemies, and even former prostitutes. Enemies called him hypocrite and prostitutes praised him for his smarts and politeness. The Governor took full responsibility and acknowledged he gave his detractors the ammo to bring him down.

In my opinion, the movie was interesting, well made, but in the end I still have no idea why this man did what he did. You can't simply say he had a manly-man's libido. Nor can it be explained by saying he had an ego larger than the world's largest condom factory that lulled him into a false security, or that he thought himself above the law.

The Governor knew right from wrong. In fact, as Attorney General he even closed down a prostitution ring. So why would anyone in his place do something he knew to be illegal? Did he emotionally implode? Subconsciously did he want to get caught? Did he act out some deep seeded turmoil by rebelling against his father while trying to figure out what he should expect of himself?

Although I don't have a degree in psychology, in my opinion, the Governor lost his Sense of Self because of the haunting shadow of an overbearing parent. The personal Sense of Self that keeps every individual grounded and needs to be the foundation of every life, was not to be found. The Governor seemed to have a sense of someone else's self. In the long-term it cost him, his family, and those who believed in him dearly. He acted out, repressed emotions, and eventually allowed subconscious emotions to explode.

Along the way to the Executive Mansion he forgot to ask himself "who am I?" Not Eliot the lawyer, Attorney General, or Governor just Eliot the person. He made someone else's expectations his own.

Bill Clinton's presidential scandal is likely to have its origins in being an adult child of an alcoholic parent. Left unaddressed this burden carries with it a whole list of demons that in his case acted out in the almost obsessive need to be liked and loved.

You may not be planning a run for governor or president, yet everyone is influenced by upbringing and social conditioning. We are die-hard Mets, Yankees, or Red Sox fans. Success is widely perceived by the house we live in, type of car we drive, or the fancy clothes we wear. You know – we want to dress to impress, see and be seen, be the go to person.

A local newspaper where I live regularly runs photos under the caption "Were you seen at ..." They're high profile events often involving fancy fundraisers or cocktail parties. Although as an aside, considering how goofy some of these folks look after what appears to be one too many cocktails, I'm not so sure I'd want to be seen. But I digress.

High powered events are a chance to look good, feel important, and be among the movers and shakers. Your mom can boast at her coffee klatch about your success. Mom will make the other mothers so jealous!

Know yourself. It sounds easy and simple. But if you are honest, it's not. It should be a life time's exploration that makes us think, reflect, transform, and transcend. It is a daily sojourn. This speaks to spiritual health and wellness.

Understandably, society is quick to condemn someone for greed, hypocrisy, arrogance, double-standards, and other crimes against the universe. A loss of self can occur at any time, and for any length of time. It explains why good people can often do some very dumb things. This doesn't excuse greed or bad behavior. But it should challenge us to find a deeper understanding for why it exists in someone.

In many ways greed, for example, is a form of insecurity. There is something very primitive linked to greed. There is a survival instinct. Greed is an extreme need to feel secure. Some subconsciously delude themselves into thinking greed chases away fear. It can lead to materialism which is a false sense of security. Security, emotional and spiritual, can only come from within.

Maybe someone is greedy because it builds an emotional wall between them and whatever threats they perceive. Or perhaps having more money the safer someone feels in an ever changing world. Often we take comfort and find security in things whether a large personal library, a huge bank account, or acquiring and accumulating things not needed. There is a fine line between having things to enjoy and using them for escape and deriving emotional security from them. The need for shelter and food can become grossly exaggerated. If Bernie Madoff knew what he knows now – the destruction of his family, would he have reigned himself in?

No doubt some of you are thinking that you don't let nice things control you. I've heard people insist that they are not controlled by possessions. The next time someone is in your home or office and admire a framed print or desk toy – give it to them. It's time to let it go and let someone else enjoy the item.

Think about getting a small, hardly noticeable scratch on the car. Considering the drama that some people would have because of it I'm not convinced. It's a car. It's a scratch. Big deal. It still starts and runs well.

Keep focus on your dignity and the dignity of others as human beings. Let me reiterate. It provides a fuller, better understanding of why colleagues are abusive or do illegal or unethical things. It also provides for a healthier way of living and interacting with others. Don't undervalue the empowerment of humility. Don't be quick to judge. Ask questions. Ask why. It can be enlightening.

Corporate scandals are reported by the media almost every day. Bribes, false advertising, and price gouging are among the many problems.

Credit card companies engage in legal yet unethical practices. Due to the necessity to have a credit score, credit cards are an important means to build a credit rating. It's no longer a choice. Setting interest rates is a choice. Setting a 29% or higher interest rate for the working poor or struggling middle class raises serious questions about the values of who sets the rates. This is an ethical issue.

Is this a fair exchange between company and consumer? Why would an ethical person, a good parent, devoted spouse, set such a policy that can lead to decades of indebtedness for someone who may least afford it? Yes, there is free choice not to use the card, assuming it's easier to build credit scores in other ways. There is also free choice how management sets interest rates.

In 2012, two Albany, NY investment brokers in their 60s were accused of scamming their clients out of millions of dollars. In light of their age, did they ever stop and think what will my son, daughter, niece, or nephew say about me in my eulogy? Of course no one will bring up the indiscretion, but it will probably be on the minds of many people. Were they successful human beings?

Did they ever stop and do a check-in and ask "Who am I and what the hell am I doing?" They lost site of the big picture and themselves. What happened to their identity? There are laws, rules, and regulations controlling this industry. The safeguards in place did nothing to protect investors. Nor did they think about the long-term consequences to clients, their families, or themselves. The blind, mindless pursuit of greater wealth, especially at someone else's expense whether it be scamming customers or urging clients to buy risky stocks to plump up a yearend bonus, speaks to fundamental issues of self and spiritual wellness.

Leona Helmsley built an upscale hotel empire, but will perhaps unfairly, always be remembered as the "Queen of Mean." She had exceptional business acumen. Yet how many people are aware of her charitable foundation? After her death she left several billion dollars to it. Clearly, she was a successful business woman, but was she a successful human being?

The examples cited involve individuals with a lost Sense of Self. They projected or acted out personal demons or had unaddressed mental health issues that should be considered. These are high profile examples. There are also ordinary folks all around us who struggle with the exact same issues on a much smaller level. The boss or colleague who finds it necessary to verbally abuse someone says more about himself than he realizes. It is unresolved personal issues being projected onto someone else. It's a form of acting out.

If there are to be solutions for ethical missteps there must be an understanding of what drives people. The human face of ethics regarding those who write policies and develop marketing strategies and those who are impacted should not be overlooked.

If someone doesn't have Sense of Self, the chances are he or she is failing as a person at certain times, in the short-term, or the long-term. It reminds me of a Hasidic reflection a seminary colleague shared with me that made a lasting impression. It's a spiritual challenge. Be "true to your Creation" *and* "to the Creation of others."

By letting experts condition us into making a distinction between business ethics or political ethics and our own personal values individuals consciously or subconsciously think there are different sets of rules. Yet in using different rules things eventually collide. All of us need to step back and reflect.

Pay for the Lifestyle or Support Your Values
At some point a board director or member of management may become aware of something that is unethical or at the very least pushing the envelope. It may be staff bullying, sexual harassment, marketing deception, or financial improprieties.

What do you do? There is a legal or fiduciary duty as a board director that may not carryover to staff. Board members, independent of any ethical issues, have clear legal requirements to be engaged and good stewards of the organization. Yet staff may have firsthand knowledge of a hostile work environment or learn through a secondary source that financial irregularities are occurring by senior management.

Are you prepared to resign as a board director or leave a job due to an unethical workplace despite the social and financial fallout? Do you have the wherewithal to be a whistleblower? If you took a blind eye to sexual harassment, would you do the same if it happened to your son or daughter? Remember the advice of Weston Smith who asked students if they were strong enough in their belief system to walk away from it. Concern about paying for one's lifestyle choices and life's basics are two very different sets of pressures. Too often we forget to make the distinction. Driving a BMW or a Ford Focus serve the same function and are equally dependable in providing transportation. Downsizing the McMansion to something more affordable may get the snooty neighbors snickering when you leave Exclusiveville, but you'll still have your dignity, character, and the basics to put food on the table, drive a dependable vehicle, and have safe, though modest shelter over your head.

Of course this can be easier said than done, yet it is very important to have exit strategies and not be lulled into letting a lifestyle own you.

Quiet Car
Amtrak's Albany-Rensselaer train to and from New York City's Pennsylvania Station often has a "quiet car" during the week where talking is not allowed, cell phones are silent, bored and chatty children are unwelcomed, and any conversations with a colleague are to be whispered and kept to a minimum. It's wonderful. You can look up from something you're working on to see the might and majesty of the Hudson River as the sun rises to give it a soft sparkle and a mystical, soothing allure.

There's an awesomeness and special kind of spirituality looking out the window observing the rolling Hudson, the Empire State's life blood during any of the four seasons. It is an opportunity to center before arriving in one of the world's greatest and busiest cities. It is critical to have times like this to nurture a Sense of Self.

Not long ago I signed up, due to professional necessity, for a Twitter account (Twitter.com/PJesep). It's a remarkable medium that I quickly came to respect. And I fear it. It is a good kind of fear. As I continue to marvel at and learn about the personal and professional opportunities using it, I'm increasingly protective of my personal needs for quiet, peace, stillness, and solitude. Even before the arrival of social media the world had become smaller and busier. It's easy to get caught up in the moment. It's easy for that moment to become minutes and then hours. It's easy for the quickened passage of time to disempower each of us.

How can a manager, executive, or any person find dwindling opportunities to mentally, intellectually, and spiritually process to reflect on life, work, and purpose? Of course there are decisions that have to be made on-the-fly, but where's the quality time to ask questions that shape values? "Do I treat my staff with respect? Do I take the time to mentor? Am I open to constructive feedback? Do I take out my personal frustrations or personal insecurities on staff or colleagues? Why do I micromanage? If I can't trust the person to do the job he or she needs to move on.

If you bring it back to ethic scandals, both legal and non-legal, it is worth exploring how different things might be if people slowed down the train they're on to listen to themselves think and ask why.

Consider the following:

Why did you eat a half pound of Chocolate?

I had a bad day at work.

Why did you have a bad day at work?

My colleague, who is never dependable, dropped the ball, and I had to do his job. The boss doesn't care. She just wants the job done.

Why are you letting your colleague win and compound your frustration?

I'm not!

You're eating the chocolate which will make your butt bigger. Why not accept the situation that he's not a good colleague and plan accordingly? Maybe this way you won't binge eat as much.

There are certain realities you can't change, so you need to manage them as best as possible. Rather than let frustration get the better of you it's more beneficial to stop, think it through, and manage the situation. Of course this is easier said than done. It takes practice and lots of it.

Learn to "craft" the right questions about your personal and professional life on your journey in searching for answers. Life's journey is now. It doesn't start after you get married, earn a MBA, get a prized promotion, graduate with an associate degree, or become a partner at a law firm.

You need to "craft," not simply ask questions. These crafted questions must be specific to you or the organization's situation. It will enable you to move beyond the surface and probe more deeply. In finding what drives you for good or ill, you will explore a deeper perspective about your place in the world and in the organization. It can have a direct, positive impact on better serving clients or customers. It can broaden your outlook in a different kind of way.

Ultimately life, whether living it in a personal or professional setting, is about asking the right questions and journeying into answers, resolutions, or serving as a basis to ask deeper questions. We know as leaders, managers, and in our personal lives to ask questions of others to do our jobs. Yet we seem to ask far fewer questions of ourselves. Either we're too busy asking necessary questions of others, or uncomfortable asking certain questions of ourselves, or we haven't developed a technique to ask questions of ourselves.

After asking ourselves questions and answering honestly, it is important to make the necessary changes in conduct and actions. You need a realistic action plan. Otherwise, as Dante warned we enter hell which is an endless conversation with ourselves. Everything requires balance. Ask. Answer. Act. Move on.

Ethics and SOS Ethics is Simple

In *every situation* the basic principles of ethics are simple. The application of ethics may be difficult, but the basics are not complicated.

The Rotarians have a very simple ethical standard. It is basic and still all encompassing. If you don't know much about them then please find out more. They're probably one of the best civic organizations in the world. Rotarians use the Four Way Test that gives them all the ethics needed in private and professional life. Some of my fondest memories are belonging to New England's largest Rotary in Portsmouth, NH.

Herbert J. Taylor created the Four Way Test in 1932. It's timeless:

1. Is it the *truth*?
2. Is it *fair to all* concerned?
3. Will it build *goodwill* and better friendships?
4. Will it be *beneficial to all* concerned?

Each test can be explained with an additional paragraph, but that's it! It can be applied to one's personal life and every profession, and be a key component to every ethics policy. Ask yourself what's it all about? Truth. Respect. Fairness. Do you really need Meta, Legal, Deontological, or Consequential Ethics to understand such basic values?

Should your spouse's expectation that he or she be treated with respect and dignity be any different than how staff or colleagues are treated by you? Should the honesty and dependability you bring to a personal relationship be any different than the virtues you bring to a professional setting? Should the sense of fair exchange you or your family expect in a commercial transaction be different than what customers expect through your company's marketing strategies? Ethics must have a sense of wholeness or universality to them.

In researching this book I reviewed many sources and the work of numerous experts. One included a near 500 page narrative that threw around words and phrases like "moral intensity," "objective measurement," "legitimate power," and "referent power." Of course there were boxes, circles, tables, and rectangles to thicken the book forcing me to give the caffeine and eye drop industry a financial boost.

Maybe it's me, but this stuff makes me yawn and roll my eyes. Is all this necessary? If so, it will cost you 90 bucks! Cha-ching! A used copy runs about $35. Less Cha-ching

I reviewed another book purchased used. Buy it new at $172. Cha-ching! Cha-ching! Cha-ching! The near 1,000 page text of my used copy arrived with the faint odor of cat urine on it (and for good reason). Toothpicks to keep the eyelids up didn't come with this tome. Kitty's calling card did the trick. The book contained wisdom about "moral imagination," "prodromal crisis stage," and "unintentional amoral management." Do we really need another language for ethics other than words or phrases like "be fair," "show respect," "don't take advantage," etc.?

Don't get me wrong there are some books on ethics worth the investment. I haven't found many, though there are some and they don't require you to give up your first born child to buy them. I wanted to throw out the kitty-perfumed book both because of the smell and its uselessness, but feared cats would howl by the dumpster much of the night.

Ethics, despite the books, seminars, or thick policy manuals can be as simple as the Rotary Four-Way Test. There are also other simple, but substantive approaches.

Christians have the "Golden Rule" – treat others as you'd like to be treated. Wiccans follow a creed of "blessed be" and "do harm to none." Baha'i has the Crown of Virtues to determine if you're a noble soul. These include bravery, happiness, kindness, politeness, honesty, patience, helpfulness, and being loving. Buddhists seek transcendence from the illusions like the false security and pleasures of materialism of this world while seeking to share and thus receive positive Karma.

Similarly, though different in other ways, Hindus also have Karma believing what you put out into the universe will be returned to you. It's a bit like the Golden Rule with a twist – knowingly hurting or profiting at someone's expense is bad energy released into the cosmos to be returned to you with interest. Do right by others and you'll be rewarded.

Caroline Stoessinger, author of *A Century of Wisdom: Lesson's From the Life of Alice Herz-Sommer, the World's Oldest Living Holocaust Survivor*, identified several lessons. My interpretation: Don't return hate. Find meaning in anything you do. Persevere no matter the situation. If you're spiritual, value something that exceeds the burdens of the mundane, the painful, the superficial, and the false security of wealth. Don't whine or make others endure your pity fest. No matter where you're at in life stay focused on the big picture.

What every person needs is a short, basic set of values to live by at all times – Sense of Self (SOS) Ethics. What's yours? Your SOS Ethics needs to be short and basic. It needs to be your mantra. It needs to be integrated in everything you do in your family, career, or relationships. As you journey in life it will need to be reviewed and perhaps revised. Be vigilant. The same applies to a standard policy in the work place. Our professional and personal lives may not always be as simple as we would like, yet more times than not we just need to keep it simple.

Let me share my personal approach to ethics. It's shared as another example, not unlike the Golden Rule or Rotary Four Way Test, to consider. HCF or GCF (Higher Power/God, Conscience, and Family). I answer to God and conscience first and foremost. And by family, I mean the one you make. It's not your parents, mother-in-law, or best friend since high school. I answer to God and conscience and since I don't have a significant other I don't go beyond those two. This is not to dismiss my close friends, or my brother, or father, but I don't live someone else's expectations.

HCF

Don't get caught up with over intellectualizing what higher power means. Nor confuse higher power with organized religion. Belief in a higher authority is not interchangeable with religion. You can believe in a pure, higher goodness, but not belong to a particular faith or denomination. You can be an atheist, agnostic, or humanist and still be very spiritual.

However you embrace or accept a higher power, even if it is a beloved grandparent who has long since passed, look to the source as a guide or moral compass. At the very least think of someone you most admire or someone famous who has made a positive, sustained difference in the world.

Belief in a higher power has nothing to do with guilt. Guilt is not a moral compass. It is not what should keep you grounded. It is not healthy. Most of us have been conditioned to think if we do something wrong "God will punish me." Think again – the earth won't crack open and demons will not pull you into the pits of eternal damnation for doing something wrong. You will have to live with yourself and that could be worse. In addition, get over yourself – God, Goddess, or the Supreme Being has a universe to run.

If you do something out of fear of punishment then it's done for the wrong reason. If you do something out of an expectation for future reward then it's done for the wrong reason. Do it because you want to be true to the best you are and can be as a child of the universe. If I'm a creation or an extension of some higher power of purity, truth, compassion, etc., I want to do the best I can to live up to this greater form of goodness.

Bad breath, sagging cheeks, scruffy face, and bloodshot eyes aside … can I look at myself in the mirror each morning? You've heard the expression when two people who are close and have a fight ask: "Are we ok?" Ask yourself "Am I ok with me?" Are you proud to be who you are and how you behave?

You are probably familiar with the Rudyard Kipland poem "If." It's a classic with a timeless message worth re-reading from time to time. I've made a modification at the end.

If you can keep your head when all about you
Are losing theirs and blaming it on you;
If you can trust yourself when all men doubt you,
But make allowance for their doubting too:
If you can wait and not be tired by waiting,
Or, being lied about, don't deal in lies,
Or being hated don't give way to hating,
And yet don't look too good, nor talk too wise;

If you can dream – and not make dreams your master;
If you can think – and not make thoughts your aim,
If you can meet with Triumph and Disaster
And treat those two impostors just the same:
If you can bear to hear the truth you've spoken
Twisted by knaves to make a trap for fools,
Or watch the things you gave your life to, broken,
And stoop and build'em up with worn-out tools;

If you can make one heap of all your winnings
And risk it on one turn of pitch-and-toss,
And lose, and start again at your beginnings,
And never breathe a word about your loss:
If you can force your heart and nerve and sinew
To serve your turn long after they are gone,
And so hold on when there is nothing in you
Except the Will which says to them: "Hold on!"

If you can talk with crowds and keep your virtue,
Or walk with Kings – nor lose the common touch,
If neither foes nor loving friends can hurt you,
If all men count with you, but none too much:
If you can fill the unforgiving minute
With sixty seconds' worth of distance run,
Yours is the Earth and everything that's in it,
And – which is more – you'll be a [successful human being]!

I don't live someone else's expectations. I don't need someone's approval. I answer to the higher authority and my conscience. In the end, I need to live with myself and be true to my creation as I understand it. No, this doesn't mean I get to do something because it feels good. I don't get to indulge or rationalize in bad behavior because it can have a negative impact on someone or on my personhood. I may not hurt others. I must respect my creation as I respect the creation of others. Neither my or the other person's creation should be taken for granted.

One time I heard an individual say he didn't think of his relationship with his spouse as being a family. Make no mistake you don't need children, furry and four legged or two legged, to be a family. Two people who make a commitment to one another have created a family. If children are involved the family has expanded.

How does or could your decisions impact your family? Sometimes a decision may not necessarily impact the other individual, but could well impact you both as a unit.

Think about whether the marketing strategy you helped to craft is honest. What if the attorney general in your state determined it wasn't? What message does it send to your friends, spouse, or children? It's not solely about you. Don't put yourself, your family, or friends in a position of awkwardness or embarrassment.

God, conscience, and family (GCF) may not resonate with you. It's not meant to, but if it does, great. If it doesn't, hopefully it provides you with a modest perspective for you to draw from when crafting and living a personal and professional mission statement.

The reason why the world lacks unity,
and lies broken and in heaps,
Is, because man is disunited with himself.

Ralph Waldo Emerson

4. Develop Your Own SOS Ethics

"Work hard, Play hard" is not SOS Ethics. It doesn't speak to your depth as a person. It just means you have a good work ethic and you enjoy the fruits of your labor. It isn't, however, an ethical foundation. You are far more than a job no matter how good you do it or how important it is. Your personhood isn't defined by the number of toys you've been able to afford. Go back to the earlier observation – take everything away. Who are you? There has to be a solid foundation before you build social, professional, or educational success on it.

Things to Consider

SOS Ethics is better than chicken soup for the soul! It leads to awareness about yourself and your place in the world by making the right personal and professional decisions. It makes you feel good about yourself and your place in the world. Soup might taste great, yet it will be gone at some point. Mentally conditioning yourself with SOS Ethics mindset will sustain you for a life time.

The world gets crazier by the day. Today more than ever there is a need for SOS Ethics that satisfies the need to make sense of the world. This overlaps with spiritual health and wellness. Bliss is finding joy in all we do, without compromising who we are or doing it at someone else's expense. It includes our personal as well as professional lives to make us complete. It is about standing proudly in our own truth. Standing proud in one's truth means you show genuine respect to colleagues you may not like, give credit for a job well done to a colleague who wouldn't do the same, and being mindful that marketing and business decisions impact families and individuals. These are some examples of ethics with a human face.

All around us we see bad people doing bad things and getting away with it. We see nice people following the rules and finishing last. "Me first and screw the rest" and "scam the system" are mantras that have been around for a long time. Today, however, they have an almost cult following.

Even good, honest, and dependable people can be drawn into doing things that don't reflect their values or principles because they need to survive in an unfair world where a level playing field is less common.

Here are things to consider as you develop your SOS Ethics. This is hardly a comprehensive list.

- Everyone would like to think they're basically a good person. Write down why you are a good person. No one will read the list. How do you treat staff or colleagues? As an executive, what tone do you contribute to the organization's culture? Why are the business practices you develop fair to consumers or clients? Are they fair to your family?

- If someone was brutally honest how would he or she describe you? Include both the positive and negative.

- Take away every material success. Who are you as a person?

- How do you hold yourself accountable? What are your expectations of yourself to do the right thing and to correct a wrong to which you may have contributed? Do you hide behind the organizational veil?

- Summarize in a few short sentences your core. What are your core, fundamental values?

- If you find the last part a bit frustrating to boil down think about the Golden Rule or Rotary Four Way Test.

- Once you've come to a basic mission statement about your personal ethics think about how they are applied in everyday life.

- Think about the last twelve months. What needs to be adjusted? Where did you succeed? Where did you acquire perspective?

- An unexpected bill, spilling coffee on your clothes when driving, and getting into a minor fender bender on the way to work all in one day is not a big deal. If you need a reality check Google poverty in Africa or the lack of freedom in Iran or human rights abuses in China. What's good in your life and why?

- Give burdens up to the cosmos. What will be will be. The "woe is me" victim gig gets tired after a while. No one wants to listen to it. Seek outside help if you need to whine all the time. Whining is not good for the soul and it prevents you from discovering SOS Ethics for everyday living.

- You're entitled to have a pity fest once in a while when you lose a job, have a break-up, or serious fight with a significant other. You're human. It's okay to have a "woe is me" moment or two, but don't make it a short- or long-term method for coping with life. It is helpful to vent and move on. You've heard this before and it's worth repeating – life is too short. Don't wallow in a pointless, self-destructive exercise.

- Looking back on any situation or parts of your life is fine. But don't stare. Do it for knowledge. If you start to stare you'll get into the pointless conversation of "if only I had done …"

Remember, reflect on the past and learn from it, but don't relive it. Applying the lessons is wisdom.

- Yesterday is gone forever. Don't waste time with "what ifs?" Today is real. There is a lot of merit to the cliché "live in the moment." Plan for tomorrow, but with the full understanding it may never arrive.

- Curiosity did kill the cat. No one likes a busy body. Don't interfere or interject yourself in business or personal settings that don't involve you. Remember everything is not about you. Don't think you need to offer an unsolicited opinion every time. There's something to be said for "economy of words" and remembering you are more likely to be listened to when you offer thoughtful counsel. If you're a busy body it say a lot about you.

- If you're trying to solve everyone else's problems whether in the office or in personal life you need to ask why. You can't do it and it's not healthy to try. Focus on yourself.

- Don't judge. Not judging the bad acts of others does not excuse them, but it may force you to be sympathetic or empathetic toward someone behaving improperly because of divorce, insecurity, job loss, alcohol abuse, abused childhood, or mental health issues, etc.

- You must listen as well as hear. Don't think about what you plan to say before the other person has stopped talking.

- Do you have conversations with others or are you talking at them? Think about it.

- Some people just have to be kept at arm's length. They can't help but project their issues onto you. Don't get angry. Try not to get annoyed. Some people, including close family members as well as those in the work place, need to be managed and kept at a distance.

- Some, perhaps many, bad people get away with bad things. Get used to it. It's life. It doesn't justify you doing the same.

- Less qualified people will get a job or, make more money than you. It's life. Get over it. Don't go down the road, it is unfair. You'll end up in the ditch of the spiritual highway.

- If you lost a high-powered job and ended up working in a place that paid you a little more than minimum wage, would you be ashamed or embarrassed? Why? What's to be ashamed or embarrassed about when making an honest wage? It may not sustain the lifestyle you once had, but that's a very different issue. If you are worried about what others will think, you've lost a Sense of Self.

- Life just is. Don't think of it as fair or unfair. Don't lament over challenges or bad situations. Don't pity yourself because someone who works less and isn't ethical has done much better than you. Don't try to understand it. If you try to it will drain energy that can and should be used elsewhere. Life just is.

- Find joy in each day no matter how small or bad your day has been. Admire a tree, stop at a bookstore, buy flowers for yourself, listen to a bird chirp, or have a really good piece of chocolate. Many joys in life are free or cost little, but are taken for granted. Savor the moment. Savor the joy.

- Live and let live. Holding a grudge in the workplace or personal life is draining and serves no purpose.

- Don't argue with God. You can't win. The greatest thinkers, theologians, and philosophers have all tried to figure out why bad things happen. Why do children die of cancer? Why are families homeless and living in cars? No one has ever come up with good explanations for why bad things happen to good people. Let it go.

- Be fair – even to people you don't like and who wouldn't be fair to you. It doesn't show weakness to be fair or to give credit to someone you work with for a good idea. Imagine if Members of Congress behaved this way?!?!?

- Take time on a regular basis, but no less than once a year to ask: "Who am I without my titles, degrees, and status symbols of success? Who am I without my job? Who am I without my personal things? If all I had were the modest clothes on my back and no car, job, house, stocks, savings account, or college degree, who would I be?"

- Attachment to things like shoes, books, clothes, music collections, etc. is false security. The only security you have comes from within. Nothing else can make you emotionally safe and spiritually grounded, but yourself.

- Don't be afraid to take intelligent risks. If things don't work out the way you hoped, you will not be executed at dawn. Nor will your family or friends think less of you. If they do, they're not much of a family and you need to get better friends. And don't forget you answer to a higher source and conscience, first and second respectively, before anyone else.

- All you have in the end is your good name. Once your reputation is soiled by your actions it's tough to clean. Don't blame the company or the work environment if it happens. Empower yourself to do the right thing.

- Don't give anyone a reason to dislike you, especially in a professional setting. Stay clear of certain conversation topics, especially in the work place.

- Life isn't an appetizer. It's the main course. Dig in. Remember your table manners. There's enough to go around for everyone. Don't be a glutton, especially at someone else's expense.

- Never try to succeed at someone else's expense. You'll regret it in old age.

- Don't assume someone who leaves an organization on bad terms has ended his or her career. Your paths may cross again soon or many years later. It's remarkable the comeback people can make. Be respectful and don't take joy in someone's downfall even if deserved.

- You define your personhood, in part, by reactions to life's successes, perceived unfairness, or the bad behavior of others. You won't always react in a manner that's true to your creation, but try to be mindful of it.

- You make your own reality. Your responses and reactions to life and its challenges are your own. No one can take away your reality.

- If someone has made you feel bad about yourself, it is your fault because you allowed it. Only you can let someone make you feel bad. Toughen up.

- Life is experience. It's perspective. If you see life through a prism of mistakes then don't get out of bed in the morning. There's a lot of perspective waiting for you. Get ready for it. Life is a long journey about self-reflection, knowing who you are, and keeping yourself grounded in your personal and professional life. If more people did it there would be fewer ethical problems.

- There will always be people brighter, better educated, and more attractive than you. Get over it. But remember you are no less valuable. You are as special and yes, pardon the cliché, beautiful on the inside as anyone else. If you think differently you have made a choice to sell yourself short.

- Don't live someone else's expectations. Duty or responsibility is not the same thing as living your life a certain way due to social conditioning or the allowing someone else's definition of success to be imposed on you.

- Without a Sense of Self you are incomplete as a person and professional.

- You cannot grow personally and professionally without a Sense of Self.

- Without a Sense of Self you cannot be a successful human being.

- You cannot hear yourself when the technology is on all the time. Turn off stereos, Twitter, Facebook, Blackberries, televisions, and the cell phone. You can do it for an hour. Find stillness.

- If you do not have a Sense of Self in a professional environment you may become part of the ethics problem we see in society today.

- You can be ethical and successful even though it is a dog-eat-dog world. You don't have to mistreat people or play one member of staff off another to get them to perform.

- Don't underestimate the value of being successful as a human being. It doesn't have anything to do with success in business or romance.

- Conscience - Did the action taken cause you angst? Why? Can you look yourself in the mirror every day knowing that you took a certain action and this will be part of your legacy? If this action or behavior, no matter how small you think it is in the greater scheme of things, is remembered after you've passed from this life would you be pleased?

- Sure, you won. You succeeded! At what price?

- Family - How does your action or inaction impact your family? Will it have a financial impact? Will it impact them emotionally? Will they be proud of you?

- What would you like your colleagues to remember most about you should you take another job?

- Be happy when someone else succeeds even if they're not the most likeable person. Ask yourself why you feel a bit of satisfaction when someone fails.

- You don't have to like someone to respect their personhood.

- Whether in private or professional life never lose focus on the big picture.

- An absence of humility often leads to problems. Very smart people do very dumb things because of arrogance or not having the personal or professional security to admit error.

- Denial, avoidance, and especially rationalization coupled with hubris is destructive. Don't hide behind a corporate veil or an organization's culture. Don't hide behind an industry standard because "everyone else was doing it." You can set a new, better standard!

- Don't forget to ask why? Why are you angry or frustrated and is your outlet to manage or address these feelings a healthy one?

The bullets shared above are some of the life lessons that I've encountered along the way. I'm still learning to apply them. They do tend to come up often.

Have you ever thought about writing down for a child or grandchild some of the dos and don'ts in life? They help shape our outlook. Sometimes certain experiences don't always shape us in a positive way. We can become jaded or defeated. Write everything down. Put the things that can hold you back to one side. Stay focused on the positive.

What values, philosophy, perspectives, and Sense of Self can collectively bring about a greater awareness – a new way of looking at things? If you spoke before a college or high school graduating class about life and lessons learned what would you tell them? The previous bullets should suggest that ethics don't start with policies, but how we see ourselves and conduct ourselves in life and toward others.

Golf & Ethics Go Together Like: Love and Marriage or a Horse and Carriage

Even if you're not a golfer please don't skip this section. Even for a non-golfer like me there's something to learn. And if you are a golfer this will affirm or refresh what you already know and perhaps get you to think and apply lessons differently.

Walter J. Travis, Editor and Jason Rogers, Associate Editor of the *American Golfer* wrote an interesting piece titled "Golf Ethics" many, many years ago. In it they observed "Of all games which disclose the petty weaknesses of human nature … its frailties … on the one hand, and sterling, manly attributes and admirable qualities of true sportsmanship on the other, golf stands pre-eminent." They added that all a person's "best and worst traits are luminously brought forth and exposed to view in all their nakedness."

It's ironic, despite so many corporate executives playing golf, that they or their companies are often cited for ethics violations. Golf has a cachet of respect, civility, fairness, collegiality, and transparency. Why do those who violate ethics in the corporate sector still honor them on the holy green when playing golf? Compartmentalization.

Let me be up front. I'm a lot like Drs. Frasier and Niles Crane from the sitcom Frasier. Although I am not a fussbudget, Lincoln Center is the second holy land for me. For the longest time I thought Tiger Woods had something to do with a Winnie the Pooh story I missed as a child. Like the Crane men, if there ain't a big-chested, full-figured lady belting out a Wagnerian aria for the next five to six hours wearing a Viking helmet and holding a spear I'm not much interested. And yes ... German can be the language of love ... in its own quirky kind of way.

So why write about golf? Personally, I don't get it. You hit a synthetic ball with a metal stick and walk around sweating while you pull a bag or drive to another hole in a tiny little car that would make a Shriner jealous. You do so for pleasure or because you must negotiate a deal, impress someone, or release frustrations (sexual or otherwise). Or maybe you just want some down time to think.

Attempts at humor and my ignorance aside, I do know golf is about people, camaraderie, and sportsmanship. It can be about improving life skills.

Sure, you're looking to close a deal sometimes or get a job on the sacred greens. But in the most basic sense golf is about trust, relationships, and personal chemistry. There is more ethics going on at a golf course than you can ever read in some silly, overpriced textbook where the authors use bizarre terms to talk about truth and trust that no longer sound like truth or trust. Golf, like ethics, is about people. Both have a human face.

I've only attempted to play golf once, which involved hacking up large pieces of turf to the horror of my friend and his club colleagues. I also remember those enjoying cocktails at the club house marveling at how someone, even a beginner, could be so inept. But I digress again. Despite this unpleasant experience I still have a positive regard for golf. What quickly comes to mind is that it can teach more about life then a laborious, over-priced ethics book or seminar. It can bring out the best in a person or perhaps highlight what kind of person the player may be as a colleague.

It requires the mind to focus. It develops patience, and with patience comes a greater likelihood you'll think things through and not react. Personal relationships are strengthened. Friendships are made on the golf course.

Golf teaches the player to make choices. Short, long, aggressive, or otherwise the player must focus and solve a problem. In contrast, an eight-hundred page ethics book is more likely to make the MBA student daydream. The lines on one's hands become fascinating. No one cites or quotes golf rules all the time. Golf has more to do with self-competition and being a better player than surpassing a colleague.

Prospective employers assess candidates for a job or promotion on the greens. They don't care if he or she hits a home run (oh, sorry that's baseball). I mean the prospective employer doesn't care about the hole-in- one (unless he or she has to buy a round of drinks later). The future employer will care if the candidate is an arrogant victor or shows no regard for other players.

In the end, it's up to the individual. The player becomes a good or bad sportsman. In the workplace the senior executive helps define the culture. It is the individual who develops marketing strategies or a senior executive who signs off on them hiding behind the organizational curtain if it is cited for wrong doing.

You may still think the world works in a certain competitive way. If you want to play and win you have to do things in a ruthless manner to win or survive. Perhaps, but is it worth it? And is it always the case? No one need succeed at someone else's expense.

Board members have the power to be more engaged, to ask more questions, to have concerns and recommendations recorded in the minutes. They need not wait for someone inside the organization to suggest a new governance practice. They can learn things by playing with middle and lower managers. Board members must be proactive if an ethical culture is to thrive and be sustained.

Similarly, staff can raise questions to superiors about the spirit of policies in place not being honored or that the values and philosophy of fairness toward a client or consumer are taking a backseat. Of course every workplace environment is different. Situations and difficult people need to be managed.

One of the most challenging environments to contend with is when professional expectations run contrary to your sense of fairness. What do you do in such a situation? If it's cultural then, assuming you want to fight the fight, expect glacial changes. Making suggestions in an understated manner is often a good approach.

How you change, manage, approach, or market things can be guided by remembering ethics has a human face because behaviors and decisions impact people. Ethical indiscretions are rarely victimless.

Integrity has no need of rules.

Albert Camus

5. Building Blocks – Bringing It All Together

Approach ethics from a stand point of human nature and it is not surprisingly that people do bad things. A person who commits an ethical indiscretion could be living someone else's expectations, are controlled by the insecurity of greed, or fail to look at the big picture and see the impact policies or marketing strategies may have on families and individuals. They may be controlled by social status and standing rationalizing the selling of risky securities to investors.

It all speaks to a Sense of Self. Who am I? This is directly connected to spiritual health and wellness. The authentic self is not something to take for granted. It can be easily pushed aside if career or wealth aren't kept in perspective. Remember the often used remark, "You've changed." Change does not always have a positive outcome when success is involved.

Spiritual health and wellness speaks to a drive to find meaning and relevance that is independent of material success with a focus on personhood and our place in the world and relationship to one another.

Authentic self and spiritual health brings success as human beings. It's the kindness, compassion, and restraint toward judgment that is shown to others. It's the humility to know that there is always someone wiser, smarter, more educated, or better connected. It's the effort to show respect to a difficult colleague as a person without compromising personal standards. It's taking responsibility whether one is a board member or senior executive or someone on the frontline.

Spiritual health and wellness, successful human being, and authentic self should heighten awareness that ethics has a human face. Ethics is flesh and blood. And when all of these elements come together then Ethical Living has begun.

You are ethics. People are ethics. Ethics has a human face.

*Live in such a way that you
would not be ashamed to sell
your parrot to the town gossip.*

Will Rogers

Appendix A

SOS Ethics Workbook

This section will help you develop Sense of Self Ethics while underscoring that ethics has a human face. It will further assist you in your quest for ethical living in every part of your life. It will be second nature. Be honest with yourself. No one need see your responses. It is something for you to reflect on and use on a regular basis.

Read all the questions or directives in this Appendix before putting pen to paper.

1. Write down at least 8 of the most positive life-lessons you've learned that you'd be willing to share with a group of college or high school graduates. "Trust no one" is not a positive life-lesson.

   1.

   2.

   3.

   4.

   5.

   6.

   7.

   8.

2. Name at least 3 people living, dead, or famous you respect. Former GE CEO Jack Welch, Archbishop Desmond Tutu, your grandmother, etc. would be examples of some of the individuals who would merit respect because of their integrity, fairness, high ethical standards, etc.

   1.

   2.

   3.

3. List some of the virtues or qualities you admire about them?

   1.

   2.

   3.

   4.

   5.

4. Give at least 3 examples how you incorporated their values or emulated them in your everyday life. If you haven't, why?

   1.

   2.

   3.

5. If you were to move on to another job what would people remember most about you? Were you mean or verbally abusive? Were you fair and tough? Were you someone others respected? Did you take credit for someone else's work?

6. List three individuals who annoy or irritate you. Perhaps there are some you don't professionally respect. Just use their initials and after them list some of their characteristics.

   1.

   2.

   3.

7. Do you respect their personhood? You don't have to like them. You don't have to respect them as professionals. Do you respect them as human beings despite their possible mental health issues, unresolved personal demons, or other limitations?

8. If you could change something about your workplace regarding its ethical culture what would it be? Have you attempted to set a standard for others to emulate? Leadership isn't a title. Leaders often set an example even if they don't have the authority. What examples do or can you set?

9. Have you ever participated in writing a workplace policy or marketing strategy? Did you ever think about how it would directly and indirectly impact actual people? Was the policy fair to all concerned? Was it beneficial to everyone?

10. Are the standards in the workplace the same for everyone? If you are a board member or senior executive are you allowing a double standard? If you are unaware of its existence do you take the time to know the organization from top to bottom?

11. Have you ever done a check-in with yourself? Think about the last 6 months and write down a summary. Think of it as a journal in retrospect. Write a stream of consciousness. Don't worry about punctuation or complete sentences. How many family dinners did you miss? Is it really worth it? What's most important?

12. It's summer. Assume the house next door is on fire. Yours is next. Stay calm. Everyone you love and your pets are safe on the sidewalk. You're the last one to leave. The fire fighters estimate that in 10 minutes or less the fire will spread to your house. What would you take? Why?

13. Write a short biography about yourself without referencing your career, degrees, or social status. Highlight any charity work, acts of kindness (preparing food for an office colleague who lost a loved one), etc.

14. What does this biography say about your values and beliefs? If someone else read it, what could they conclude?

15. Go back and re-read what you've written in each question or directive then summarize your life-philosophy? Boil it down to a handful of simple terms.

16. Going forward how can and will you change your approach in the workplace and in your private life?

17. How can you better integrate your personal values with your conduct in the workplace?

18. Write a short, succinct paragraph that is your code of conduct for Ethical Living in your personal and professional life.

*Even the most rational approach
to ethics is defenseless if there isn't
the will to do what is right.*

Alexander Solzhenitsyn

Appendix B

Are You Living Ethically?
Are You On the Right Path?

Yes or No

1. Do you think about how a decision, internal policy, or marketing strategy may directly impact a client, customer, or colleague? Do you attach a face or see the human element to potential outcomes?

   _____

2. Do you consider personal and professional ethics distinct?

   _____

3. In the past 12 months do you know of a friend or colleague who made an unethical decision due to pressure by a client, customer, or supervisor?

   _____

4. In the past 12 months has there been direct or indirect pressure on you to compromise your personal or professional ethics by a client, customer, or supervisor?

   _____

5. Does a culture exist in your organization where it is possible you'll be asked at some point to do something unethical by management or a client?

_____

True or False

1. Ethics is about perception. _____
2. Ethics is about respect. _____
3. Breaking the law is always unethical. _____
4. If someone methodically obeys the law he or she is ethical. _____
5. Ethics work best when they are identified in different capacities and kept distinct such as social, personal, and by profession (legal ethics, medical ethics, etc.). _____

On a scale of 1-6 answer the following questions.

1 – Strongly don't agree.
2 – Don't agree.
3 – Uncertain
4 – Not applicable.
5 – Agree.
6 – Strongly agree.

1. Professional ethics work on paper, but not in reality. _____
2. I have a very clear understanding of ethics in the workplace. _____
3. There are too many types and definitions for ethics. _____
4. A new approach is needed to ethics in the workplace and/or working with clients. _____

5. Ethics is too generic or theoretical to have practical value. _____

6. Ethics is too complicated and policies are not user friendly. There has to be an easier way to approach things. _____

7. If you want to keep a job or expect to be promoted you must keep personal and professional ethics separate. _____

8. More and better quality ethics training is needed at my organization. _____

9. A greater connection between ethics and legality is necessary. _____

10. Senior management or the board of directors is disengaged regarding ethics. _____

11. The level of commitment to ethics by management directly impacts office morale, my productivity, and how I do my job. _____

12. My company is committed to the highest ethical standards. Management does not give ethics lip service. _____

13. I have been subject to workplace bullying or have seen it at my current place of employment. _____

14. Bullying is a problem at my office. _____

15. Bullying is not a major problem at my office, but there are issues that need to be addressed. _____

16. Sometimes I wonder if pressure at work or from home makes me sometimes bully a peer or subordinate. _____

17. Ethics policies and protocols internally and externally can be improved at my organization. _____

18. My organization needs better trained ethics officers or human resource personnel when it comes to ethical issues that arise in the workplace or in dealing with clients or customers. _____

19. My organization is too small to have a designated ethics officer or for human resources also to be trained in ethics, but there is still a need to consult someone in the area. I need a reliable resource. _____

20. If a major client or customer pressured me to do something that was by all objective standards unethical my organization would back me up when I refused to do it. _____
21. If I was asked or expected by senior management to do something unethical, though probably legal, to please a client, I would resign. _____
22. Most books and articles on ethics are not useful. _____
23. As part of my efforts to stay on top of needs and changes in my profession I read at least one ethics book a year and articles on a regular basis. _____
24. My understanding of ethics is likely to change as the nature of my business or profession changes. _____
25. Several times a year I read self-help books to benefit me personally and at work. _____
26. Spiritual wellness is as important as mind and body health. _____

Analysis

Yes or No

1. If you answered **no**, give this further consideration. Ethical breaches can have serious consequences and can even include injury or death. Imagine a company lobbying against greater safety laws for miners insisting there are enough laws on the books. Think about a marketing strategy that doesn't disclose pertinent information to the consumer. Put a beloved family member in the place of the client when following company policy.

2. If you answered **yes**, ask yourself how values of respect, honesty, etc. change from a professional setting to private life. Should they?

3., 4., and 5.

   If you answered **yes** to two or more questions then it's time to have an exit strategy and not be complacent about it. Things aren't likely to improve. If you (your friend or colleague) are forced to do something unethical and in the remote chance it became public, you can't plead the defense of pressure. In addition, once you do something unethical you've bought into the culture.

True or False

1. **True**. Even the perception of wrongdoing can be detrimental to an organization. Never give someone a reason to doubt or question something that's going on. The appearance of something even though innocent can have negative consequences.
2. **True**. Respect your clients, customers, and colleagues. You don't have to like them to respect them. Treat them with the fairness you expect for yourself. Remember the Golden Rule.

3. **False**. A pregnant friend is in your car and goes into labor. Do you come to a full stop at the stop sign or slow down and roll through it? Brave men and women of conscience hid and saved Jews during World War II breaking Nazi laws. Brave men and women of conscience hid runaway slaves in America breaking federal law in the United States.
4. **False**. See above.
5. **False**. Although there are unique challenges specific to certain professions, in all cases ethics pertains to people and relationships. A customer wants value for his or her money, a client expects his or her attorney to be honest and prepared, an investor expects not to be sold a high risk product by a trusted stockbroker, and the list goes on. Respect, honesty, and fairness are some of the basic elements that should be found across the board no matter the situation or profession.

On a scale of 1-6 answer the following questions.

The answers to these questions can give you and your organization valuable data. The answers may provide you or your organization a starting point. They offer opportunities for discussion while identifying issues that could lead to potential problems. In some cases, such as whether your organization would back you if you refused to comply with a client's request to do something unethical, will help determine how long you should stay at the organization. There were also a series of questions about bullying in the workplace. Bullying can occur by a low level staff member who believes he has power for some reason and it can occur by a supervisor or one peer to another. The answers to these questions merit special attention.

I am different from [George] Washington;
I have a higher, grander standard of principle.
Washington could not lie. I can lie, but I won't.

Mark Twain

Bibliography

Achakulwisut, Atiya. "Happiness as a Choice in Life." Bangkokpost.com. February 21, 2012.

Barton, Ruth Haley. "Spiritual Direction with Pastoral and Corporate Leaders." *Journal of Spiritual Direction*. Presence. Vol. 16, No. 2 – June 2010.

Benefiel, Margaret. *The Soul of a Leader – Finding Your Path to Success and Fulfillment*. New York: The Crossroad Publishing Company, 2008.

_____. *Soul at Work – Spiritual Leadership in Organizations*. Church Publishing, New York: Seabury Books, 2005.

Bessant, Judith. "Ethical Behavior More than Just about Following Rules." *National Times*, November 30, 2011.

Bentley, Paul. "Nice Guys Really Do Finish Last ... Nasty People Earn $10,000 More a Year, Study Finds." DailyMail.co.uk. August 15, 2011.

Bloxham, Eleanor. "What's at the Core of Corporate Wrongdoing?" CNN.com. December 29, 2011.

Bose, Praveen. "Q&A: Robert F Bruner, Dean, Darden Business School." Business-Standard.com/India. October 27, 2011.

Boukre, Vernon J. *History of Ethics – Volume 1 – Graeco-Roman to Early Modern Ethics*. Mount Jackson, VA: Axios Press, 1968.

Buscaglia, Leo. *Born for Love*. New York: SLACK Inc., 1992.

_____ *Personhood – the Art of Being Fully Human.* New York: Fawcett Columbine, 1982.

Campbell, Joseph, ed. *The Portable Jung.* New York: Penguin Group, 1976.

Carroll, Archie B. and Ann K. Buchholt. *Business & Society – Ethics and Stakeholder Management – 7th Edition.* Mason: South-Western Cengage Learning, 2009.

Carroll, Linda. "Where Harassment is Higher, So Are Salaries." MSNBC.com, November 30, 2011.

Ciulla, Joanne B., Clancy Martin, and Robert C. Solomon. *Honest Work – A Business Ethics Reader.* New York: Oxford University Press, 2007.

_____. *History of Ethics – Volume 2 – Modern and Contemporary Ethics.* Mount Jackson, VA: Axios Press, 1968.

Cohan, William D. "Did Psychopaths Take Over Wall Street?" Bloomberg.com. January 3, 2012.

Collins, Denis. *Essentials of Business Ethics – Creating an Organization of High Integrity and Superior Performance.* Hoboken: John Wiley & Sons, Inc., 2009.

Crotty, Ann. "Watchdog Unable to Police Ethics." IOL.co.za. May 3, 2012.

Dubinsky, Joan and Alan Richter. "Global Ethics and Integrity Benchmarks." CorporateComplianceInsights.com, 2009.

Ellmann, Liz Budd. "Tending to Spirituality in the Workplace." *Journal of Spiritual Directors International.* Vol. 7: No. 2 – June 2001.

Ferrell, O. C., John Fraedrich, and Linda Ferrell. *Business Ethics – Ethical Decision Making and Cases – 2009 Update – 7th Edition*. Mason: South-Western Cengage Learning, 2010.

"Former Corporate Executive Warns Students Not to Cross Ethics Lines." Mississippi State University News Bureau. February 1, 2012.

"Four-fold Increase in Ethical Investments Over Last Decade." LiverpoolDailyPost.co.uk. April 26, 2012.

Gandon, Richard. "Understanding the Mortgage Meltdown – What happened and Who's to Blame." MoneyMatters101.com. May 4, 2012.

Gardiner, Beth. "Business Skills and Buddhist Mindfulness." WSJ.com, April 3, 2012.

Garside, Kevin. "Lee Westwood proud of Golf's Ethics and Moral Values After Elliott Saltman is Handed a Three-Month Ban." Telegraph.co.uk. January 19, 2011.

Glover, Hubert D. "Drawing Lessons from Our Ethical Failures." BusinessFinanceMag.com, October 26, 2011.

Gordon, Claire. "With Bonuses Slashed, Wall Street is In Crisis." AOL.com. February 6, 2012.

Grantham, Jeremy. "Capitalism has No Sense of Ethics or Conscience." InvestmentNews.com. February 28, 2012.

Grohol, John M. "Self Esteem and a Sense of Self." PsychCentral.com, March 17, 2003.

Gulf Coast Business. "Successful Businesses Can Also Be Ethical Ones." Al.com. April 4, 2012.

Hechinger, John and Mark Niquette. "Penn State's Shame from Abuse Scandal Threatens College's Rise." BusinessWeek.com, November 11, 2001.

Hicks, Donna. "The Ten Temptations to Violate Dignity." FoxNews.com. November 6, 2011.

Hopcke, Robert H. *A Guided Tour of the Collected Works of C.G. Jung.* Boston: Shambhala, 1999.

Institute for Business Ethics and Social Responsibility. "What is the Difference Between Personal Ethics and Professional Ethics?" May 12, 2010. Centers.SCB.RIT.edu.

Jesep, Paul Peter. "Symphonic Leadership Eyes Goal, Not Process – Modern Team Management Misses." *Portsmouth Herald* (NH), June 3, 2001.

_____. "What about the Lawyers?" Examiner.com. December 15, 2011.

Joffe-Walt, Chana and Alix Spiegel. "Psychology of Fraud: Why Good People Do Bad Things." NPR.org. May 1, 2012.

Joseph, Joshua. "Ethics in the Workplace." SAECenter.org. October 2000.

Kaye, Leon. "A New Era of Ethical Leadership?" GreenGoPost.com, November 9, 2011.

Kim, Susanna, "10 Things We Didn't Learn from Enron Scandal." News.Yahoo.com, November 29, 2011.

Kirschenbaum, Howard and Valerie Land Henderson, eds., *The Carl Rogers Reader.* New York: Mariner Books, 1989.

Kristula-Green, Noah. "Our Secret Service Needs More ... Aristotelian Ethics?" TheDailyBeast.com. May 1, 2012.

Leloup, Jean-Yves. *Being Still – Reflections on an Ancient Mystical Tradition.* New York: Paulist Press, 2003.

Lopatto, Elizabeth. "Wealthy More Likely to Lie, Cheat: Researchers." Bloomberg.com. February 28, 2012.

MacDonald, Chris. "Banks, Image Problems, and the Ethics of Lobbying." CanadianBusiness.com, October 27, 2011.

MacKenzie, Gordon. *Orbiting the Giant Hairball – a Corporate Fool's Guide to Surviving with Grace.* New York: Viking, 1998.

Marks, Norman. "Why CFOs Shouldn't Leave Ethics to HR." www.3.cfo.com. May 2, 2012.

Maxwell, John C. *Ethics 101 – What Every Leader Needs to Know.* New York: Center Street, 2003.

McLeod, Saul. "Carl Rogers – Self Actualization." SimplyPsychology.com, Published 2007 (retrieved February 28, 2012).

Mhonderwa, Bradwell. "Zimbabwe: Ethics Enhance Competitiveness." AllAfrica.com. March 27, 2012.

Mishra, Akshaya. "We are Among the Happiest, Does that Surprise?" FirstPost.com/India. February 11, 2012.

Moment, Robert. "7 Principles of Admirable Business Ethics." SBInformation.about.com. (printed April 5, 2012).

Norman, Jan. "45% Have Witnessed Workplace Misconduct." OCRegister.com. January 23, 2012.

Norris, Kyle. "Homeless Writers Find Meaning, Sense of Self." MichiganRadio.org. (retrieved February 28, 2012).

Oxley, Michael and Bart Stupak. "Ethical Warning Looming in U.S. Workplaces." MarketWatch.com. January 23, 2012.

_____. *There's No Such Things as Business Ethics.* New York: Warner Books, 2003.

Pearlstein, Joanna. "Why We Lie, Go to Prison and Eat Cakes: 10 Questions with Dan Ariely." Wired.com. June 22, 2012.

Peppers, Cheryl and Alan Briskin. *Bringing Your Soul to Work – An Everyday Practice.* San Francisco: Berrett-Koehler Publishers, Inc., 2000.

Piff, Paul K., Daniel M. Stancato, Stephanie Cote, Rodolfo Mendoza-Denton, and Dacher Keltner. "Higher Social Class Predicts Increase Unethical Behavior." Proceedings of the National Academy of Sciences (PNAS.org). February 27, 2012.

Quast, Lisa. "How to prevent Poor Ethical Decision-Making." Forbes.com. December 19, 2011.

Rich, Jennifer. "Mixing a Little Spirituality in Your Business." Bradenton.com, November 10, 2011.

Riely, Kaitlynn. "Educators to Share Strategies on Ethics." Post-Gazette.com. May 3, 2012.

Rogers, Carl. *On Becoming a Person: A Therapists View of Psychotherapy.* New York: Mariner Books, 1995.

_____. *A Way of Being.* New York: Mariner Books, 1980.

Rohr, Richard. *The Naked Now – Learning to See as the Mystic See.* New York: The Crossroad Publishing Company, 2009.

Rosenthal, Phil. "Mistakes of Enron Repeated Again and Again." ChicagoTribune.com, December, 4, 2011.

Rubin, Gretchen. "Carl Jung's Five Key Elements to Happiness." PsychCentral.com. February 25, 2012.

Ryan, Liz. "Why Corporate Ethics Statements Don't Work." BusinessWeek.com. May 18, 2012.

Schoeman, Cynthia. "Turning Around a Morally Bankrupt Company." IOL.co.za. April 11, 2012.

Scott, Matthew. "Compliance and Ethics Movement Takes Off." CorporateSecretary.com. November 9, 2011.

Sewake, Bianca. "Albers to Host Ethics Day." SU-Spectator.com, April 12, 2012.

Sen, Amartya. *On Ethics & Economics.* Malden: Blackwell Publishing, 1988.

"Sheila Bair on Keeping Banks Honest." BillMoyers.com. July 13, 2012.

Sherren, Joe. "Ethics and Culture." TheGuardian.pe.ca. April 7, 2012.

Sinetar, Marsha. *Ordinary People as Monks and Mystics.* New York: Paulist Press, 2007.

Smith, Greg. "Why I Am Leaving Goldman Sachs." NYTimes.com, March 14, 2012.

Spencer, Amy. "Happiness Secrets: 7 Ways to Make the Best of a Bad Day." HuffingtonPost.com, February 17, 2012.

Sternberg, Robert J. "Essay on Why Smart People Make Foolish Ethical Choices." InsideHighered.com. November 9, 2011.

Stoessinger, Caroline. "My Take: 7 Life Lessons from a Holocaust Survivor." CNN.com. April 19, 2012.

Teen, Mak Yuen. "Is Success a License to Cheat?" TodayOnline.com. November 10, 2011.

Tolstoy, Leo. Walk in the Light and Twenty-Three Tales. Farmington, PA: The Plough Publishing House, 1998.

Tvedten, Brother Benet. *How to be a Monastic and Not Leave Your Day Job.* Brewster: Paraclette Press, 2006.

Van Hecke, Madeleine L. *Blind Spots: Why Smart People Do Dumb Things.* Amherst (NY): Prometheus Books, 2007.

Welch, Jack and Suzy Welch. "Jack Welch Elaborates: Shareholder Value." BusinessWeek.com, March 16, 2009.

> Wright, John. "Despite Woes, Conflicts, World a Happier Place than in 2007as 22% (+2 points) of Global Citizens Say They're 'Very Happy'." www.ipsos-na.com. February 9, 2012.

Zingales, Luigi. *A Capitalism for the People: Recapturing the Lost Genius of American Prosperity.* New York: Basic Books, 2012.

_____. "Do Business Schools Incubate Criminals?" Bloomberg.com. July 16, 2012.

*You must learn to be still in the midst of activity
and to be vibrantly alive in repose.*

Indira Gandhi

About the Author

Paul Jesep is founder of Entrepreneur Spirit (www.EntrepreneurSpirit.biz), a service for individuals, nonprofits, and small to mid-sized businesses with a focus on ethics analysis and development in the workplace. Paul blogs on ethics and spiritual wellness for Examiner.com. Independent of Entrepreneur Spirit, Paul provides organizational and one-on-one spiritual health and wellness counseling and direction for professionals through Corporate Chaplaincy (www.CorporateChaplaincy.biz). He is a member of Spiritual Directors International. Paul earned degrees from Union College, Western New England University School of Law, the Graduate School of Political Management at The George Washington University, and Bangor Theological Seminary. Paul served as an Ethics Officer for an organization with over $1 billion in economic impacts, and may be contacted through Entrepreneur Spirit or Corporate Chaplaincy.

www.EntrepreneurSpirit.biz

www.CorporateChaplaincy.biz

www.ingramcontent.com/pod-product-compliance
Lightning Source LLC
Chambersburg PA
CBHW061512180526
45171CB00001B/143